FREEDOM IN CHRIST *Discipleship Series*   **BOOK 2**

WIN THE
DAILY BATTLE

RESIST AND STAND FIRM IN GOD'S STRENGTH

STEVE GOSS

D1051982

MONARCH
BOOKS
Oxford, UK & Grand Rapids, Michigan, USA

Published by Monarch Books
an imprint of
Lion Hudson plc
Wilkinson House, Jordan Hill Road,
Oxford OX2 8DR, England
www.lionhudson.com/monarch

ISBN 978-1-85424-858-9

First edition 2008

Acknowledgments
Unless otherwise stated, Scripture quotations are taken from the Holy Bible, New International Version, © 1973, 1978, 1984 by the International Bible Society. Used by permission of Hodder and Stoughton Ltd. All rights reserved.

A catalogue record for this book is available from the British Library.

*This book is dedicated to my wonderful wife Zoë,
whose very name (Greek for 'spiritual life')
speaks of the ministry that God has given us together.
There is no way I could play my part in that ministry
without her constant support, hard work, words of
real wisdom and willingness to step out in faith.*

Contents

A Special Word of Thanks

I have learned just about everything I know about helping people become fruitful disciples from Neil Anderson, author of *The Bondage Breaker*, *Victory Over the Darkness* and many other books. These are now regarded by many Christians as classics, and rightly so.

It has been my immense privilege to spend time with Neil, to sit under his teaching at many conferences, to collaborate with him in writing *The Freedom In Christ Discipleship Course*, and to have the opportunity to put my questions to him while we were 'on the road' together.

One of the first things I did when I sensed that the Lord might be prompting me to write this series was to ask Neil if he minded. After all, the way he has taught these great biblical principles of freedom is so much part of me now that I could not possibly write these books without using his fundamental methodology.

He had every right to say no and, if he had done that, I would have dropped the project there and then. However, he positively encouraged me to get started.

For that, and for all he has taught to so many over the years, I am indebted to this man of God who continues to travel the world with this life-changing message.

My thanks go too to Tony Collins and Rod Shepherd at Monarch for their help in getting this series off the ground, as well as to the fantastic team at Freedom In Christ Ministries for their constant support and sacrificial service in taking this message to churches around the country.

Foreword

For twenty-five years I believed in God and regularly attended church. If anyone asked me about my beliefs, I told them that I was a Christian. I looked like a Christian and generally acted like one. In Europe and North America if one respected their parents and wanted to be a 'good boy or girl' it was the cultural thing to be and do. It is sobering to look back and realize that I was one of those millions of cultural 'Christians' who don't have an authentic relationship with their Creator and Heavenly Father. If God hadn't intervened in my life I would have become like the rest of those disillusioned by religion and joined the pagan parade now exiting the culturally or politically correct 'church'.

Religion is the curse of this world, and the force behind many of the conflicts plaguing the planet. However, a relationship with God is our only hope. I was the senior warden of an Episcopal (Anglican) Church and working as an aerospace engineer when I was invited to attend a lay institute for evangelism. I didn't know what that was and had I known I probably wouldn't have gone. The priest wanted me to go with him. So I did, and while learning to share my faith I realized I didn't have any. The presenter asked what difference it would make in our religious beliefs if Christ hadn't come in the flesh? I didn't have an answer. I believed in God and that was enough. Wasn't it?

I heard the gospel for the first time, and gladly gave my heart to Christ and was born again. I became a new creation in Christ, but it took me several years to fully understand what that really meant. At first I was really excited about my new-found faith, and at the same time disappointed in myself for playing 'church' all those years. I couldn't help but wonder how many others were going through the same motions and missing the real relationship that God wants us to have with himself.

Two years later I sensed the call of God to go into full time ministry. The past forty years have been an exciting adventure of learning, growing, and discovering how God sets captives free and binds up their broken hearts. My dear friends and colleagues, Steve and Zoë Goss, have been going through the same transformation and now God is using them to accomplish his work in the United Kingdom.

In writing these four discipleship books, Steve has done a masterful work in presenting the core message of Freedom In Christ Ministries. You will learn, as we have, what difference Christ makes in our 'religious beliefs'. Jesus is the One who died for the sin that has separated us from God. Jesus rose from the dead in order that we can have new life in him. His sacrificial life, death and resurrection also disarmed the god of this world (Colossians 2:15). Jesus came to undo the works of Satan (1 John 3:8) who has deceived the world (Revelation 12:9), and has it under his control (1 John 5:19).

The Church is not an institution for religious observances. It is not an organization, it is an organism. The Church is the body of Christ. The membership is made up of born-again believers who are alive and free in Christ. Their names are written in the Lamb's book of life. 'As many as received him, to them he gave the right to become children of God, to those who believe in his name' (John 1:12). You will discover this and much more as you work your way through this series of discipleship books. So welcome to the family of God. You have many spiritual brothers and sisters in Christ who are learning and growing just as you are. "The Holy Spirit is bearing witness with your spirit that you are a child of God" (Romans 8:16). Have you ever considered what an incredible privilege it is to be called a child of God? The grace of God is truly amazing, and may you grow in that grace and become all that your Heavenly Father created you to be.

Dr. Neil T. Anderson
Founder and President Emeritus of Freedom In Christ Ministries

Win the Daily Battle

As a child I used to love snowball fights, the bigger the better. It was the nearest I could get to a real battle experience – there was real ammunition and you could score real hits. In every battle, one side would eventually be overwhelmed by the other and would suffer a relentless bombardment of snow and ice, leaving them drenched and cold. Very often at that point, one or more of them would stand up and say, 'We don't want to play any more.' That was, of course, designed to bring the game to a close and stop the onslaught – not that it always worked!

I can only imagine the fear faced by soldiers in a real battle as the firepower against them seems to become overwhelming and they are in constant fear of death. If only they could stand up and say, 'I don't want to play any more' and bring it to an end. But they can't. Once they are in it, they have no option but to see it through to the bitter end.

When you became a Christian, I doubt that you realized that you were entering a spiritual war zone. Perhaps all that had been talked about up to that point was love, peace and joy. Yet the battle between good and evil runs like a thread all the way through the Bible. Satan makes his first appearance right at the start in the Garden of Eden itself. He also pops up at the beginning of Jesus' ministry. And much of the Book of Revelation describes the mighty battles to come.

If you are a Christian, you are in the battle whether you realize it or not – and, for that matter, whether you like it or not. Just like in a real battle, choosing not to play is not an option.

One of the most quoted Chinese people of all time is an obscure military commander who lived around 500 years before Christ. Sun Tzu wrote a series of essays on the art of war, packed with pithy statements full of wisdom. His texts are still used in military training around the world.

One of his sayings was, 'The supreme art of war is to subdue the enemy without fighting.' In the spiritual battle, our enemies are trying to do just that to us. They are trying to make us ineffective without our even realizing they are there. If we do not understand that we are in a battle, we will not fight and it will be easy to subdue us.

What does it mean for a Christian to be in a spiritual battle? Is it a real battle? If so, who or what are we fighting? Is it possible to become a casualty or are Christians somehow immune?

This book is designed to answer those key questions. It will explain the nature of the battle we are in and how it works. Once we understand the nature of the battle and the incredible resources we have at our disposal, we will see that there is no reason at all why we should not win this daily battle and that there is nothing whatsoever that can stop us becoming the people God wants us to be. However, if we do not understand these things, it is difficult to see how we can avoid becoming a spiritual casualty.

Know Yourself, Know Your Enemy

I am especially struck by the relevance of another of Sun Tzu's often-quoted observations to the battle faced by every Christian every day:

> *If you know the enemy and know yourself, you need not fear the result of a hundred battles. If you know yourself but not the enemy, for every victory gained you will also suffer a defeat. If you know neither the enemy nor yourself, you will succumb in every battle.*

In the spiritual battle, knowing both yourself and your enemy is essential. Every defeated Christian I have come across either does not understand who they are now that they are a Christian or who their enemy is – in most cases, in fact, they don't understand either very well. When they come to understand these things and resolve outstanding issues, however, they are able to move on and become fruitful.

If you don't know who you are in Christ, you won't know what your capabilities are. You might give up when you could press on through to victory. If you don't know your enemy, you might run away thinking he is stronger than you, when in fact it may all be deception.

So, how can we get to know ourselves and our enemy? We could do a lot worse than turning to Paul the Apostle for some help. He addresses these things in the letter he wrote to the church at Ephesus. In Ephesians 2:1–10, he paints a clear picture of what we used to be like before we were Christians and how different we are now, and spells out for us exactly who our enemies are (there are three):

13

As for you, you were dead in your transgressions and sins, in which you used to live...

If we are to know ourselves as we are today, we need to understand where we come from and what we used to be like. This is a 'before and after' passage and Paul begins here to describe the 'before' picture. Note that he uses the past tense.

He says that we were dead. Now, you may from time to time struggle to get up in the morning. You may even appear a little comatose over breakfast. But, if you are managing to read this book, it is safe to say that you are not dead according to the generally accepted definition of the word – and never have been. Clearly Paul is giving the word some other meaning, and in fact he talks about sins in which we used to *live*. How can we live if we are dead?

When God made Adam, he gave him a physical body, his outer person. But the really important part of him was his inner person, his soul or spirit. Adam was physically alive. That simply means that his inner person was connected to his outer person. Adam was also spiritually alive. That means that his spirit – the core of his being – was connected to God.

That is how we were designed to be too: on the one hand, our spirit connected to our physical body; and on the other hand, our spirit connected to God.

Adam and Eve were told, 'you must not eat from the tree of the knowledge of good and evil, for when you eat of it you will surely die' (Genesis 2:17). They did eat. Did they die? That's the big question!

Well, they did not die physically – at least not for several centuries. But they did die spiritually. The connection that their spirit had to God was broken and they were separated from God. This 'spiritual death' is what Paul is talking about, because Adam passed that condition down his family line to every one of his descendants – including you and me. We were all born physically alive but spiritually dead.

It was Adam's connection to God – his spiritual life – that had given meaning to him. It meant that he was intrinsically significant, and he knew it – he was in intimate relationship with God himself. He was absolutely secure: God provided all his needs and protected him from danger. He was completely accepted: he would have known nothing but the most amazing love surrounding him.

Let's get back to Paul:

> As for you, you were dead in your transgressions and sins, in which you used to live when you followed the ways of this world.

The kind of life Adam had is what you were created to have too: perfect security, the highest significance, 100 per cent acceptance. But that was not the life you were born into. From our first breath we have not had the spiritual connection to God that we were meant to have. Yet we were created with those inbuilt needs for security, significance and acceptance that spiritual life would have fulfilled.

The result is that all of us instinctively try to meet those needs. That's why we naturally 'followed the ways of this world'. The 'world' is simply the cultural system we grew up in – which will vary according to where you are from. The world presents itself to us as a friend, as the answer to our deepest needs. In the West where I grew up, for example, the world is constantly promising to meet my deep need to feel secure through finance. It promises to meet my need to feel significant by showing me how I can impress others, and to meet my need for acceptance by saying that I simply need to do what other people do so that I fit in. In fact, far from being a friend, the world is the first of our enemies.

> ...and of the ruler of the kingdom of the air, the spirit who is now at work in those who are disobedient.

Now Paul introduces us to the second enemy arrayed against us. This 'ruler of the kingdom of the air' is, of course, Satan, the devil. The Bible is clear that he is a real being who is out to thwart God's plans.

When God created Adam and Eve, the devil had to crawl at their feet in the form of a snake. They were the ones God had chosen to rule over his creation. However, Adam and Eve effectively handed over their right to rule the world to Satan when they sinned. That's why Paul calls him 'the ruler of the kingdom of the air', and we are also told that the whole world lies in his power (1 John 5:19).

As we grew up, we didn't realize that we were following Satan. But we were. He is behind the world's false promises to meet our needs for significance, security and acceptance. Just as he told Adam and Eve that they could meet their needs without God, that's been his constant message to us. In fact, all temptation is simply an attempt to get us to meet our legitimate needs for significance, security and acceptance independently of God.

All of us also lived among them at one time, gratifying the cravings of our flesh and following its desires and thoughts.

We were not just following the world and the devil. We were also influenced by what Paul calls 'the flesh', the third enemy we face.

As we grew up, especially before we became Christians, the world and the devil were constantly pushing us to cope with the legitimate needs we have in various ways – but independently of God.

Biscuits are a poor substitute for knowing you are accepted by the Living God, but they do bring temporary comfort – at least that's what I discovered as I grew up. I remember on a Saturday morning as a teenager, discovering that if I felt low, a packet of custard creams really hit the spot (and I do mean a whole packet!). I did it so often that, for me, comfort eating became a way of coping with life's pressures. Others turn to alcohol or drugs or learn to cope in different ways. These coping mechanisms soon become ingrained patterns of behaviour that are difficult to break.

The flesh is a collection of habitual ways of thinking and behaving. It doesn't just consist of coping mechanisms. There can also be negative patterns of thinking ('I'm useless', 'I'm dirty') that the enemy gets us into which then become like deep ruts in our minds. Each of us has a set of learned behaviour and habitual thought patterns which are the 'cravings', 'desires' and 'thoughts' of the flesh.

Like the rest, we were by nature objects of wrath.

This sums up the whole sorry situation. Our very nature – the essence of who we are – was displeasing to God. In fact, we were by nature an object of God's righteous anger. What is more, we were unable to do anything about it. We were without God and without hope in the world. Completely and utterly helpless.

Paul has introduced our three enemies to us so that we can start to get to know them and how they work. He has also spoken about what we used to be like. That is helpful, but to 'know ourselves' we really need to know what we are like now. So Paul turns his attention to the 'after' picture, and it is crucial. Too many Christians still see themselves as they used to be rather than as they are now.

But because of his great love for us, God, who is rich in mercy, made us alive with Christ even when we were dead in transgressions – it is by grace you have been saved.

If I were to ask you why Jesus came, what would you say? I've tried this a few times and most people say something like, 'To forgive my sins.' That is of course true, but it was not the ultimate purpose, just a means to an end. Perhaps we should let Jesus answer the question in his own words: 'I have come that they may have *life*, and have it to the full' (John 10:10).

Hmmm... What was it that Adam lost? Life. What did Jesus come to give us? Life!

In fact, when you become aware of it, you suddenly find that word 'life' appearing all over the New Testament. For example:

> *In the beginning was the Word... In him was* life, *and that* life *was the light of men.*   (JOHN 1:1-4)

> *I am the resurrection and the* life. *He who believes in me will* live, *even though he dies.*   (JOHN 11:25)

The key issue here is *life*. What Adam lost was spiritual *life* with all its security, significance and acceptance. In Christ that is completely restored. Our deep needs are fully met in Christ.

> *And God raised us up with Christ and seated us with him in the heavenly realms in Christ Jesus, in order that in the coming ages he might show the incomparable riches of his grace, expressed in his kindness to us in Christ Jesus.*

Satan may still be the ruler of this world but we have not only *died* with Christ, we have been *raised up* with him to new life and have also *ascended* with him to the right hand of the Father in the heavenly realms, the ultimate seat of power and authority in the universe.

We are not subject to Satan any more. In fact, as long as we are submitting to God, when we resist Satan, he has no option but to turn tail and run from us (see James 4:7).

> *For it is by grace you have been saved, through faith – and this not from yourselves, it is the gift of God – not by works, so that*

no one can boast. For we are God's workmanship, created in Christ Jesus to do good works, which God prepared in advance for us to do.

From being in a completely hopeless position, we are now God's 'workmanship'. The original Greek word means 'a work of art'. Deep down inside there has been a dramatic change. We are no longer by nature utterly repugnant to God. We are by nature absolutely beautiful and completely acceptable. In fact, we now share God's nature (see 2 Peter 1:4). How amazing is that!

'Remember, if it seems too good to be true, then it probably is.' That was a piece of good advice I came across regarding internet scams. Maybe it's also the reason why we find it so difficult to grasp what has happened to us now that we are Christians. It just seems too good to be true!

We are so used to being let down by offers that don't live up to their advertising that we have an inbuilt caution, or indeed, outright cynicism. But when it comes to our new identity in Christ, it really is true. You are now a saint, a holy person, completely pleasing to God.

So, if we are to know ourselves, we need to concentrate on ourselves as we are now: holy ones, children of God, pure, clean, acceptable. The first book in this series majored on that.

Although we have changed, our enemies have not. Before we became Christians, the world, the flesh and the devil were our enemies and they still are. There is, however, a difference. Back then we did not recognize them as enemies. We were happy to go along with them. Now, as we shall see, we can walk free from them.

The Battleground

So we are in a battle against three enemies – the world, the flesh and the devil. But we need to know what that means in practice. What does the battle look like?

Well, Jesus says that he is *the* Truth, while Satan is described as the father of lies. The battle is all about truth.

The *world* comes at us from the outside, bombarding us with counterfeits to truth. It sets itself up in opposition to the pre-eminence of Christ. Of the three, it is the one we are likely to find the most attractive.

The *flesh* comes at us from the inside. It sets itself up in direct opposition to the Holy Spirit (the Spirit of Truth) and his guidance, and we have to choose every day which prompting we will listen to. Of the three, it is the most pernicious and difficult to deal with because those habitual ways of thinking become so deeply ingrained.

The *devil* is constantly attacking us, usually working through the world and the flesh rather than mounting a full-on attack. As he is the father of lies, he opposes the God of all truth. Of the three he can inflict the most damage if he is allowed to.

All three of them try to subdue us without fighting. They attack us at our weak points, our legitimate needs for significance, security and acceptance. They throw messages at us designed to 'press our buttons' and exacerbate those needs. Then they offer us ways that purport to meet our needs. However, instead they simply result in our eventually being taken captive.

It's a battle for truth – but not just truth per se. Often

people quote Jesus as saying, 'The truth will set you free.' In fact, that is only a partial quote. What he actually said was, 'You will know the truth and the truth will set you free' (John 8:32). Truth on its own does not set anyone free. We have to *know* it. It has to penetrate our minds.

For example, when I was stuck in a sin–confess cycle watching the wrong sort of stuff on TV, it was true that at any time I could have put an end to that – Paul says categorically in Romans 6 that the power of sin is broken in the life of a Christian. However, it was only when I connected with that truth – when I really *knew* it in my mind – that I was able to deal with it.

The other key thing we need to understand about the battle is where exactly it is taking place. When Adam and Eve were in the garden, God said that they were not to eat from 'the tree of the knowledge of good and evil' (Genesis 2:17). Satan came along looking to wreck God's plan for their lives, and his appeal to them was at the level of 'knowledge': he questioned whether God was being honest with them and then said, 'when you eat of it, your eyes will be opened and you will be like God, *knowing* good and evil' (Genesis 3:5). They were looking for knowledge. They, like Satan, wanted to be like God and know everything.

Paul sheds some light on what was going on here when he expresses some concern that the Corinthian church might be deceived in the same way: 'But I am afraid that just as Eve was deceived by the serpent's cunning, your *minds* may somehow be led astray from your sincere and pure devotion to Christ' (2 Corinthians 11:3).

The Fall took place when Satan was able to lead Eve's *mind* astray. Much of the damage that resulted from the Fall was at the level of the mind. Far from becoming like God in knowledge, paradoxically, what actually happened was that they went from a position of knowing God in an intimate, relational way to not knowing him at all. That lack of knowledge of God was passed down to their ancestors. Paul says that, although it is obvious to anyone who looks around that God is real, people turned away from him because 'their *thinking* became futile and their foolish hearts were darkened. Although they claimed to be wise, they became fools' (Romans 1:21–22). He continues, 'Furthermore, since they did not think it worthwhile to retain the knowledge of God, he gave them over to a depraved *mind*, to do what ought not to be done' (Romans 1:28).

The original temptation to Eve was at the level of knowledge. The effect of giving in to it was that knowledge of God was lost and our thinking became futile and our minds depraved. In fact, it is our depraved minds that stop us turning immediately to God for salvation: 'The god of this age has blinded the *minds* of unbelievers, so that they cannot see the light of the gospel of the glory of Christ, who is the image of God' (2 Corinthians 4:4). The battle takes place primarily at the level of our thinking. It is a battle for our minds.

There is an old saying: 'The thought is the father of the action.' If we believe a lie, we will act accordingly. That is why the world, the flesh and the devil all direct their efforts at our minds. They try to get us to believe things that are not true. Adolf Hitler was a past master at influencing minds for evil. We may not like his methods but we can learn from them. This is what he had to say about the effective use of propaganda:

> *All effective propaganda must be limited to a very few points and must harp on these in slogans until the last member of the public understands what you want him to understand by your slogan.*
>
> *The most brilliant propagandist technique will yield no success unless one fundamental principle is borne in mind constantly and with unflagging attention. It must confine itself to a few points and repeat them over and over.*[1]

The world, the flesh and the devil act in much the same way. They appeal at the level of our emotions, claiming over and over again that they can meet our deepest needs for security, significance and acceptance. Or they repeat the same negative message again and again in different ways until we start to believe it: 'God isn't real', 'God doesn't love you', 'You are not like everyone else', 'This might work for others but not for you'.

For example, take the truth that you are now a child of God, fully accepted and loved by God. The devil may try to set up scenarios in your life that send you the message that you are useless – in fact he's been doing that to all of us since the day we were born. Perhaps a parent or a teacher said something negative to you such as, 'You're useless. You'll never amount to anything!' The enemy plays the tape over and over in your mind until the thought pattern, 'I'm useless, I'll never amount to anything' becomes part of your flesh – a habitual way of thinking. Whenever someone compliments you or an opportunity to put yourself forward for something arises, the tape plays, trying to get you to back down.

The message makes you feel bad because you were created for acceptance – therefore you desperately want to be accepted. Along comes the world, claiming to offer you any number of ways to meet that need. It may tell you that offering your body to others will fulfil the need – but in fact it just leads you into sexual bondage. It may tell you that alcohol or drugs will make you feel better – again, they just lead to bondage and the gradual breakdown of your life. It may tell you that the way you look is the key to feeling good and so on. More bondage. These things cannot deliver on their promises because they are offering routes to significance, security and acceptance that are independent of God. Only he, the God of all comfort, is genuinely able to meet those needs and meet them in full.

Becoming mature Christians involves dismantling the propaganda we have already unthinkingly absorbed and guarding against accepting any more. I am currently engaged in something of a running battle with an unknown graffiti artist. He or she comes along at night and sprays graffiti onto our office building. As soon as I find out it's there, I go along and obliterate it by painting over it. The aim of our enemies is to be able to graffiti our minds. We need to be alert and on our guard so that we can obliterate the graffiti as soon as we become aware of its presence.

Thankfully, the Lord has provided us with weapons so that we can 'demolish arguments and every pretension that sets itself up against the knowledge of God', and 'take captive every thought to make it obedient to Christ' (2 Corinthians 10:5). He has also given us his peace which 'will guard your hearts and your minds in Christ Jesus' (Philippians 4:7).

Every Christian can expect to win this battle for truth that rages in our minds. There is no one who cannot take hold of the truth and walk in genuine victory – even over those things that seem to have defeated us time after time in the past. The world cannot overcome us: 'Everyone born of God overcomes the world' (1 John 5:4). We can expect to experience daily victory over the flesh: 'Live by the Spirit, and you will not gratify the desires of the flesh' (Galatians 5:16). And, even though Satan is the one who can inflict the most damage if he is allowed to, he is also the easiest of the three to resolve: 'Submit yourselves, then, to God. Resist the devil, and he will flee from you' (James 4:7).

Now that we understand that the battle is primarily a battle for our minds, for our thoughts, let's take a look at how each of our three enemies works and what we need to do to stand against them.

NOTE

1. *Hitler's Mein Kampf*, translated by Ralph Manheim, London: Pimlico, 1996.

Our Enemies: The World

It's important to understand how the first of our enemies, the world, tries to mess up our mind. We noted earlier that it comes at us from the outside, bombarding us with counterfeits to truth. It operates in conflict with Christ and his pre-eminence and, of our three enemies, is the most obviously attractive.

The Bible uses the term 'world' in two different ways. In John 3:16, for example, it says that God loved the world so much that he sent his only Son to die for it. In that sense it is talking about the people who live in the world.

That is to be contrasted with a verse such as 1 John 2:15: 'Do not love the world or anything in the world.' This is clearly referring not to people but to the world system in which they live.

It is this world system that is our enemy. It acts against us in a number of different ways. It feeds us a complete but false view of reality – what is commonly called a 'worldview' – so that we base our decisions and actions on false assumptions. It also makes a direct appeal to our emotions by promising to meet our deepest needs independently of God.

Let's examine its main tactics.

Tactic 1: Painting a false picture of reality

As a student I read many works of literature from the eighteenth and nineteenth centuries written by authors from different cultures and countries. I remember at that time becoming aware that people's understanding of 'life, the universe and everything' – their 'worldview' – varied significantly depending on when and where they were brought up and lived. Indeed, studying French literature in particular, it was possible to track a clear move across the whole of society from a belief in God and the King as God's divinely appointed ruler to a belief that, if God existed at all, it was as the Creator but not as a God who took a personal interest in the universe.

I realized that I too was a child of my time, that many of the things I had come to take for granted as true would no doubt be overturned by future generations. I remember feeling trapped by that concept, feeling that I had no choice what to think and believe, because it was largely determined for me by the time and place of my birth. If you want to understand just how quickly and comprehensively ideas change, incidentally, try reading a fifty-year-old school science textbook. Imagine how dated and wrong our current textbooks will look fifty years from now!

It's important to understand that we all start out as 'children of our time'. We are all hugely influenced by the prevailing culture we are brought up in. We absorb ideas and attitudes firstly from our family, then from our education and also from the wider culture of newspapers, TV, the internet and so on. It's impossible not to be influenced. Some of the things we pick up from our culture are good, some not so good. In short, all of us end up with a 'worldview'. We do, however, have a choice and in Christ we are free to make the right choice.

James Sire (in his book *The Universe Next Door*) helpfully defines a worldview as 'A set of presuppositions or assumptions which we hold (consciously or subconsciously) about the basic make-up of the world.' If, however, we want to look at the world as it really is, we need to evaluate critically and carefully the thoughts and attitudes that we have picked up from our culture. That's important because our worldview acts like a filter. We pass everything that happens around us through it in order to work out what it means. It all happens without our even realizing it. But if our worldview is faulty, it will lead to faulty judgments about what happens in our life.

I liken our worldview to wearing a pair of spectacles. Two people may look out of the window at the same view. If one of them is wearing dark glasses, their view is filtered and they may conclude it is a dull day. If another of them is wearing glasses with rose-tinted lenses, they may conclude that the sun is going down. In fact, neither of those things might be true.

Have you ever seen a 3D film? In reality, these are cleverly prepared 2D films but if you put on a special pair of spectacles, your mind is tricked into believing it is 3D. You see things right in front of your nose but they're not really there. Because you are seeing the film through spectacles, your mind is tricked into interpreting it in a way that is exciting and fun but that does not reflect reality.

There is a huge variety of different worldviews. I want to look at some of the more prevalent ones around today. The purpose in doing this is to help us step outside our own worldview and begin to realize (if we don't already) that we actually have one!

A non-Western worldview

We'll start with one that is probably not familiar to most in the West – though if you were brought up in Africa, for example, this will probably be very familiar. This set of spectacles is a belief system called 'animism'. It is found in its purest form in tribal societies but is also accepted by well-educated people in most modern societies.

Most animists believe in a Creator of some kind but they tend to see that Creator as being so far removed from them that he does not play a very significant role in daily life. The animist is far more concerned with a neutral spiritual power (sometimes called *mana*) which is thought to run through everything in the universe – animal, vegetable and mineral – and with spirits of many types.

Mana is thought to be a power much like electricity. In our everyday lives, we turn switches on and off, change light bulbs and plug in extension leads, but we also have specialists in dealing with electricity because, if not handled properly, it can harm us. Whether it does good or evil depends on which wires we connect and to what. So just as we use a specialist to handle electrical installations, animists use a spiritual 'electrician' – usually called a shaman or a witch-doctor – to handle problems facing them in the spirit realm. He is the expert in dealing with this impersonal spiritual power because he knows the special formulas, activities and words necessary to manipulate it.

Animists also believe in spirit beings. These spirits are often associated with natural objects or with people who have died. They may be good or evil and have individual identities. Animists believe that humans can control these spirits if they know the right things to do and the right words to say.

This control over spirits is not complete, however, and animists live with the constant fear that they might somehow displease them and invite retribution. They also fear that an enemy may develop some superior occult skill to direct the power of *mana* or the spirits against them.

Animism is found in all parts of the world and even among those who profess to believe one of the world religions. In Thailand, where Buddhism is the dominant religion, a university professor said that he did not know a single intellectual who was not also an animist. The president of the university at which he taught regularly consulted the spirits before making major decisions. 'New Age' thinking has for some time been introducing animism into Western society too.

The Western or 'modern' worldview

Most people brought up in the West in the last fifty years or so have been conditioned to look at the world in a particular way that is usually referred to as the Western or 'modern' worldview. Although most still profess to believe in God, to all intents and purposes, in the Western worldview God is so irrelevant that he may as well not exist.

The Western worldview divides reality into 'the natural' and 'the supernatural'. God and things that go bump in the night are put into 'the supernatural realm'. This has no relation to daily life, or 'the natural realm'. We sort of believe in them but, when push comes to shove, we put our faith in what we can see, touch and measure.

The supernatural realm is seen as so far removed from the natural realm that they don't even touch. Spiritual issues are considered unnecessary for understanding life; they are therefore not an essential part of education. Religion can be left out of our children's science and humanities lessons, it is thought, without losing anything that matters.

The natural realm is thought to be governed by scientific laws. God may have created the world and established scientific laws, but he is now seated far away on his throne in heaven and doesn't tend to interfere with life on earth.

Essentially, the Western worldview says that if you can't test it and prove it scientifically, it's not true. The ordinary person who doesn't spend very much time thinking about the 'big issues' has come to believe, for all practical purposes, that the world came about by chance and God, if he exists at all, is irrelevant to daily life.

In trying to make their faith work in this environment, some parts of the church have tried to get rid of all unnecessary supernatural 'baggage' in order to fit in and appear 'normal'. That's why it's not uncommon to find ministers denying miracles such as the virgin birth and the resurrection or refusing to believe in the existence of angels and demons.

The 'postmodern' worldview

But the Western worldview has been in decline for some decades. It's being replaced by something called the 'postmodern' worldview, though perhaps when history looks back it will be given a name in its own right rather than being defined by what it comes after. So here is another pair of spectacles to try for size. Most of us brought up in the West will find that we have been influenced by both the modern and the postmodern views – the younger you are, the stronger the postmodern influence is likely to be.

Postmodernism has some of its roots in the thinking of a philosopher named Nietzsche who said, 'There are many kinds of eyes...and consequently there are many kinds of "truths", and consequently there is no truth.'

That little phrase 'no truth' sums up postmodernism for me. The Western worldview may not see God as truth but it does not deny the existence of truth itself – it sees it as something that can be discovered by science. However, in the postmodern view, there is no such thing as truth – at least not as something that stands on its own. Instead, each person is free to make up their own version of truth, and your version will depend on the community to which you belong. Since there are many human communities, there are many different versions of truth. For example, university professors report that students increasingly are not prepared to say that the Holocaust was wrong. They would readily admit that it would be wrong for them but do not want to impose their 'truth' on a different people in a different time.

If all truth is created by humans, and all humans are equal, then the logical next step is that all 'truth' is equally valid. So every individual's beliefs, values, lifestyle and perception of truth are seen as carrying equal weight and validity. The consequence of that is that any worldview that is seen to claim to have 'all the answers' is viewed with great mistrust. In fact anyone who holds strong convictions is looked at with suspicion and contempt because, since there is no real truth, those who have convictions of truth must be dangerous fanatics.

One other disturbing facet of the postmodern worldview is that it no longer differentiates between what a person thinks or does and the person himself: 'Who I am = what I do'. If you say that my behaviour is wrong you're judging *me*. If you disagree with my beliefs you're disparaging *me*. So there is enormous pressure now for us to accept everybody's lifestyle as true and valid, no matter what it is.

That is why Christians are under pressure to agree that other religions are equally valid. Saying that we respect the right of other people to different beliefs and that we are happy to have fellowship and dialogue with them, but that we draw the line at agreeing with those beliefs, is no longer acceptable. There is a pressure to agree that their beliefs are equal to our own.

In effect, postmodernism says that all truth claims are equal – except those, like Christianity, that say that all truth claims are not equal. In fact, it has been said that the one intolerance that seems to be acceptable is intolerance of Christians!

The biblical worldview: truth does exist

Which worldview is right? That there is a neutral spiritual power called *mana* that we can harness? That truth is something that only science can uncover? That truth is whatever you want to believe? Does it even exist at all?

What worldview did you absorb as you grew up? How much of it still defines your thinking? Is it possible to remove our 'glasses' and look at reality as it really is, or are we forever destined to see it through a filter, to remain trapped as 'a child of our time'?

The Bible is very clear that truth does exist quite apart from humans. In fact, as we have already seen, it teaches that God *is* truth. If God really is truth, when he tells us how it is, then that is how it is. Christians have very good reason to believe that God is indeed truth and that he has set out how it is in the Bible. If we adopt the way of looking at the world that the Bible has, then, we will have taken off our glasses.

Os Guinness wrote: 'In the biblical view, truth is that which is ultimately, finally and absolutely real, or "the way it is", and therefore is utterly trustworthy and dependable, being grounded and anchored in God's own reality and truthfulness.' The biblical worldview is 'how it is'.[1]

This is not 'blind faith'. I have been following with interest the debate between scientists who are atheists and scientists who are Christians. It is interesting to see that those who insist there is no evidence for God are in effect taking a faith position. The very existence of the universe is clearly potential evidence for God. They may have other ways of explaining it but how can they rule out the possibility that it has a Creator?

Faith and logic are often seen as incompatible but they are not. Take the postmodern position that there is no such thing as truth independent of human beings. Logic demonstrates that truth really does exist. Consider the most important question facing everybody in the world – what happens when you die?

Hinduism teaches that when a soul dies it is reincarnated in another form. Christianity teaches that souls spend eternity in either heaven or hell. Atheists believe that we have no soul and that when we die our existence simply ends. Postmodernism says that you can make up whatever you want to believe as long as you don't hurt anyone else.

Can all those things be true? The postmodernist would answer, 'Yes. It's fine for you to believe whatever you want as long as you don't attack my truth. We all have our own truths.'

But does that really make sense? To put it another way, does what you believe will happen to you when you die make any difference to what will actually happen? Or will all people everywhere have the same experience after death regardless of their beliefs?

Logic says that we will all have the same experience regardless of what we choose to believe before the actual event. If Hindus are right, we will all be reincarnated. If Christians are right, we will all stand before the judgment seat of God. If atheists are right, all of our existences will come to an end. But it's a logical impossibility that they can all be true at the same time.

So it's clear that there is such a thing as real truth that exists regardless of what an individual chooses to believe. This is the view that humankind has held for thousands of years and was taken as obvious until very recently.

In fact, because God is truth, all genuine truth is God's truth and is true everywhere for everyone all the time. Truth is true in that it is objective and independent of any human. Because it is true, it cannot contradict itself. There is, therefore, never any need for Christians to run from truth or to try to hide some fact that looks at first sight 'inconvenient' to the biblical worldview. If God is truth – and he is – then all truth is God's truth.

Do you feel that you are being intolerant or arrogant when you say that Jesus is the only way? It certainly causes the hackles of postmodernists to rise.

Yet, come back to that crucial question: what happens when we die? There can only be one true answer to it. Christians have many reasons for believing that God has chosen to reveal that in the Bible. We are not proposing a version of truth that we have made up ourselves. The biblical worldview has been tested and found reliable by millions of people over thousands of years. In fact, many of those ordinary people have found that, by choosing to believe it, they have been able to accomplish, or be a catalyst for, extraordinary things: abolishing slavery, helping drug addicts find freedom, and so on.

We may find it difficult to advance an unfashionable argument. But are we really being helpful if we encourage people in their view that there really is no truth and it doesn't matter what they believe, when Jesus has said very clearly that he is the truth and that 'No one comes to the Father except through me' (John 14:6)?

Tactic 2: Mix 'n' match

The world wants us to accept unquestioningly the worldview we grew up with. It's essential, however, that we recognize that our upbringing and experiences have led us to look at life in a particular way so that we can learn to look at life as it really is.

If we don't, we are likely to run into problems as Christians. Instead of making a decision to turn away from our old beliefs, we simply add some new beliefs (the Christian bits) to the way we look at life. This mix-and-match approach is very common and very dangerous. Each of us needs to come to a point where we realize that what we believed is so incompatible with the truth that we make a conscious decision to throw it away. Otherwise it will lead to compromise and double-mindedness and we'll be 'unstable in all we do' (James 1:8).

The danger is that, although we might say we believe what God says, our behaviour will demonstrate that we really believe something quite different. Two examples of this from Christians in animistic societies are quoted in *The Beginner's Guide To Spiritual Warfare* by Tim Warner.[2] The first was approached by another Christian because of sin in his life. Instead of thanking his friend and dealing with the sin, the man became very angry. He said, 'I will never forgive you for this. I'll tell the church that I do, because I know I am supposed to forgive; but Ingos [his tribe] don't forgive!' He was saying that he professed Christianity, with Christ as Saviour and Lord and the Bible as the final authority in faith and life, but in reality his actions demonstrated that he placed his tribal beliefs above those of the Bible.

In an East African country, an evangelical mission agency

was ready to hand over leadership of the church they had planted to African leaders. Two men were presented for the position. One of them went to a witch-doctor to secure a charm to enhance his chances of being chosen as leader of the church. What was this man saying about what he really believed? He was saying, 'I'm not sure about the power of God, but I really believe in the power of the witch-doctor.'

It's always so much easier to spot this mix-and-match approach in people of a different worldview. But what about those of us brought up in the West? We say we believe the Bible, but isn't it true that many of our decisions are made on the basis of what we can afford rather than on what God is saying? We say we believe in the power of prayer but does the way we spend our time bear this out, or are our actions really demonstrating that we believe that we can sort out our lives for ourselves and use prayer only in the last resort? How many Christians read their horoscope? More than you might imagine.

It is easy to mix 'n' match our Christian beliefs with the world's 'culture of success'. The world tells us that being wealthy will make us significant and lead others to accept us. It's easy to spiritualize a desire to be 'successful'. I have heard Christian preachers implying that the amount of money we have is a measure of God's blessing on us or our spiritual well-being. Others justify their desire for wealth by saying, in effect, 'The more I have, the more I can give away.' Jesus was very clear: 'You cannot serve both God and Money' (Matthew 6:24) – but, he said, if we seek God's Kingdom first, God will meet all our needs.

Paul has some apposite words for us in regard to the world: 'So then, just as you received Christ Jesus as Lord, continue to live in him, rooted and built up in him, strengthened in the faith as you were taught, and overflowing with thankfulness' (Colossians 2:6–7). We need to be firmly rooted in Christ in order to grow. If we are not firmly rooted, the next verse carries a stark warning: 'See to it that no one takes you captive through hollow and deceptive philosophy, which depends on human tradition and the basic principles of this world rather than on Christ' (Colossians 2:8). We are either growing in the Lord or we've been taken captive by some deceptive way of thinking. We need to work towards shedding all vestiges of the worldview we unthinkingly absorbed as we grew up in favour of 'how it is' in reality, as laid out by the Creator himself in the Bible.

Tactic 3: Promising to meet our deep needs

Our worldview is a subtle thing that at first we do not even notice. We simply take for granted that the assumptions we have come to make about the world around us are true.

However, the world also makes a more direct assault on us. It offers us what the flesh craves and what the devil wants us to believe. The world system has been firing its seductive messages at us for years, messages that tell us on the one hand that we are insignificant, insecure and nobody likes us and which, on the other hand, promise us ways of becoming the exact opposite. Ultimately it's all smoke and mirrors. 1 John 2:15–17 says:

> *Do not love the world or anything in the world. If anyone loves the world, the love of the Father is not in him. For everything in the world – the lust of the flesh, the lust of the eyes and the pride of life – comes not from the Father but from the world. The world and its desires pass away, but the man who does the will of God lives forever.*

This is a key passage in understanding how the world makes its appeal to us. It shows that there are three channels through which the world works. Translated literally, these are the lust of the flesh, the lust of the eyes and the pride of life.

We will have a look at the flesh as an enemy in its own right in due course, but here we see how linked our enemies are. I have already explained that one of my flesh habits is comfort eating, and that is always likely to remain a vulnerability for me. The world exploits that ruthlessly. I find myself bombarded with images of eating and drinking, and supermarkets and restaurants offer me a veritable abundance of good-tasting delicacies. If I'm feeling a little low, the best plan for me would be to turn to God, who is the God of all comfort. The world, however, conspires with my flesh to pull me in a different direction. It promises to meet my needs through the food on offer. But if I succumb to a bit of a binge and then another, before I know it I'm actually in bondage and it becomes much more difficult to stop.

The world works also through the lust of the eyes. It shows me things that it says will meet my needs – those legitimate needs for security, significance and acceptance that God created me to have. A poll conducted by a Christian website[3] concluded that around half of Christian men (and 20 per cent of Christian women) are addicted to internet porn. It was not a particularly scientific study in that participants were self-selecting, so the number quoted is probably on the high side, but nevertheless I can confirm from my own experience of helping Christian men that this is a major issue. That addiction starts with the world promising to meet our need for intimacy simply by our looking at naked flesh. 'What harm can it do? It's not actual physical sex,' comes the seductive selling line. Before we know it, we're returning again and again to the same sites, and it feels as if we can't stop. Again a promise of freedom turns into slavery to sin. A great deal of the world's attraction is presented through visual images: glossy magazines, TV ads and so on. Jesus said this:

> The eye is the lamp of the body. If your eyes are good, your whole body will be full of light. But if your eyes are bad, your

whole body will be full of darkness. If then the light within you is darkness, how great is that darkness! (MATTHEW 6:22-23)

Then there's the pride of life. This is simply the temptation the world throws at us to boast about our life, based on the lie that it is possessions or achievements that make us significant. I have fallen for this one again and again. As I grew up, even though I was a Christian for some of that time, I unthinkingly swallowed the world's lie that the amount of money I earned and the possessions I had (particularly what car, how big a house or what clothes) would somehow make me intrinsically more or less significant. I found myself striving for promotion, for a bigger company car, for bigger and better houses. All the time I was working for those things above God's will for my life, I was effectively neutralized in my walk with the Lord. I may still have been going to church – indeed, I was a leader in my church and even had a bit of a preaching ministry in other churches – but, despite the outward appearances, my heart was set on worldly things and there was very little real fruit. The truth is, as Jesus made clear, it is impossible to serve two masters. The world's agenda is to get me to serve it. It doesn't really mind if I am still going through the motions of being a Christian as long as my actions show where my heart really lies.

How can we tell where our heart lies?

Do not store up for yourselves treasures on earth, where moth and rust destroy, and where thieves break in and steal. But store up for yourselves treasures in heaven, where moth and rust do not destroy, and where thieves do not break in and steal. For where your treasure is, there your heart will be also.

(MATTHEW 6:19-21)

What does your mind tend to drift to in an idle moment? That's probably as good an indication as any as to where your 'treasure' is.

The reality is that those who feel the need to boast about what they have, their achievements or who they know, are very insecure people. They are using those things as a crutch to bolster their self-image. We don't need to do that any more. We are now holy and pleasing to God. We don't need to do anything more to gain God's acceptance or to have our needs met.

It's interesting to note that these three channels are the same ones Satan used when he tempted Eve and again when he appeared to Jesus in the wilderness and tempted him to follow a different agenda than the one God had given him. Often we fail to see that it is Satan who is behind the appealing but ultimately empty promises that the world makes, but he is, after all, 'the ruler of this world'.

Our defence against the world

Junk our old worldview

We need to make a radical decision to junk our old worldview and embrace 100 per cent the biblical worldview.

In New Testament times, when someone became a Christian it was much more obvious to them that they were completely changing their way of thinking. Often they would burn the things associated with their old belief system as a clear break with the past. In the Book of Acts we read of a group of people who 'came and openly confessed their evil deeds. A number who had practised sorcery brought their scrolls together and burned them publicly' (Acts 19:18–19). The value of the scrolls they burned was estimated at 50,000 drachmas – that is equivalent to well over 2 million pounds today. That is a radical decision that marks a complete change from one way of life to another.

We too need to realize that our old worldview is incompatible with the truth and make the same radical decision. It may be that you have never actually realized that you had a worldview. Why not spend some time right now with the Lord asking him to show you how your worldview has influenced your thinking, then specifically renounce it and embrace the biblical worldview 100 per cent.

Renew our minds

Paul says, 'Do not conform any longer to the pattern of this world but be transformed by the renewing of your mind' (Romans 12:2). I can't think of a Christian I know who would not want to be transformed. Often they are asking God or someone they see as an 'anointed Christian' to do it for them. This is the only place I know in the Bible that tells us how we can be transformed and that it is by renewing our minds – and we are the ones who have to do it.

Remember that the mind is where this battle is played out. The issue is truth. We are transformed as we gradually kick lies out of our belief system and replace them with truth. As we make a constant decision to reject the lies of the world and to offer our bodies as living sacrifices, we can replace the lies we have been believing with truth.

As we gradually see reality more and more from God's perspective, we will increasingly recognize the world's promises for what they are: empty. When you realize that money really does not bring you happiness and that loving money actually leads you into bondage, it becomes much easier to reject the world's appeal to you on that level.

It is helpful to analyse how we have fallen for the world's false promises to meet our legitimate needs in the past. Then we will know our vulnerabilities and can take measures against falling for the same old lies again and again. In fact, it is good to do the very opposite of what the world would have us do. If, for example, we have fallen for the lie of the world that our security comes from having money, why not instead work on turning into someone who gives money generously rather than someone who hoards it?

Maybe the world seems too big for you. The truth, however, is that 'Everyone born of God overcomes the world' (1 John 5:4). There is no reason whatsoever why we should not overcome the world and every reason why we should!

Our enemies do, however, work together, and for a complete answer to the world, we also need to know how to deal with the flesh and with the devil. There is little point in concentrating on renewing our minds if we do not also ensure that we have removed every foothold of the enemy. We simply won't be able to do it. When Jesus prayed for his disciples (John 17:15ff), he specifically said that he was not praying that God would take them out of the world but that he would protect them from the evil one. He then went on to say, 'They are not of the world even as I am not of it. Sanctify them by the truth; your word is truth.'

Truth is the key. The world bombards us with false messages about what we lack. As we conclude this section on the world, let's read in full the passage from Jesus' 'sermon on the mount' that we have already quoted extensively:

> *The eye is the lamp of the body. If your eyes are good, your whole body will be full of light. But if your eyes are bad, your whole body will be full of darkness. If then the light within you is darkness, how great is that darkness!*
>
> *No one can serve two masters. Either he will hate the one and love the other, or he will be devoted to the one and despise the other. You cannot serve both God and Money.*
>
> *Therefore I tell you, do not worry about your life, what you will eat or drink; or about your body, what you will wear. Is not life more important than food, and the body more important*

than clothes? Look at the birds of the air; they do not sow or reap or store away in barns, and yet your heavenly Father feeds them. Are you not much more valuable than they? Who of you by worrying can add a single hour to his life?

And why do you worry about clothes? See how the lilies of the field grow. They do not labour or spin. Yet I tell you that not even Solomon in all his splendour was dressed like one of these. If that is how God clothes the grass of the field, which is here today and tomorrow is thrown into the fire, will he not much more clothe you, O you of little faith? So do not worry, saying, 'What shall we eat?' or 'What shall we drink?' or 'What shall we wear?' For the pagans run after all these things, and your heavenly Father knows that you need them. But seek first his kingdom and his righteousness, and all these things will be given to you as well. (MATTHEW 6:22–33)

As we renew our minds and gradually understand deep down inside that these words really are absolutely true, we can walk free from the rubbish thrown at us by the world. We really can live as Jesus recommends.

NOTES

1. Os Guinness, *Time For Truth*, Baker Books, 2000, p. 78.
2. Neil Anderson and Tim Warner, *The Beginner's Guide To Spiritual Warfare*, Servant Publications, 2000.
3. ChristiaNet.com, August 2006.

Our Enemies: The Devil

Let's look now at the devil, the second enemy in the battle that is raging for our minds. Jesus calls him the 'father of lies' (John 8:44). In this battle for truth, he is constantly feeding us half-truths and downright lies.

The good news is that one of the specific reasons given why Jesus came is to destroy the devil's work (1 John 3:8). We noted earlier that this is the most easily resolvable of the three issues we face. However, if we do not resolve it, it is the one that can cause us the most damage.

The reason that many Christians don't resolve it is simply because they don't understand it. And that has a lot to do with the fact that our enemies work together and Satan is behind the false pictures of reality that are peddled to us by the world. Just as there are different worldviews in different parts of the world, Satan's tactics vary somewhat accordingly.

In many parts of the world – for example, in Africa – where the worldview is predominantly animistic and people see the spiritual realm as real, Satan's activities are more overt. He often manifests himself in ways that are designed to produce fear and give people the impression that he is more powerful than he is as he seeks to reinforce the false notions behind the local worldview. The message that Christians in these countries need to hear is that Satan is alive but not so dangerous as he makes out, that Christians are seated with Christ far above him, and have everything they need to ensure daily victory.

In the West, however, where the prevailing worldview wants us to dismiss the reality of the spiritual realm, Satan tends to hide himself so that people are fooled into living as if the physical world is all there is. This can lead Christians in the

West to the false view that somehow Satan is more active in other countries and that demonic activity is generally encountered only rarely in the West. The vast majority of Christians in the West agree (at least theologically) that Satan is real and that they are in a battle with him. However, influenced by the prevailing worldview, they then tend to leave that concept out of their day-to-day thinking and live their lives as if that were not the case. I constantly find myself falling into that trap.

The message that Christians in the West need to hear is that Satan is real and potentially very dangerous to us if we do not understand how he operates and what we can do to stand against him.

How powerful is Satan?

We are not given a great deal of information about Satan's origins in the Bible but it is generally agreed that he was a high-ranking angel who wanted to be like God and led a rebellion of angels against him. Of course, it failed and this resulted in Satan and the rebellious angels being cast out of heaven. They are now locked in a bitter and ultimately futile battle with God.

We have seen how Adam and Eve handed over their right to rule the world to Satan who is described as 'the prince [ruler] of this world' (John 12:31). We're told that the whole world lies in his power (1 John 5:19). Satan would like you to believe that he is of equal power to God (or at least that he is nearly equal to God) and that the two of them are locked in some kind of cosmic tug of war that could go either way. He clearly is powerful but just how powerful is he?

If you were asked to rank God, Satan and you in order of spiritual power, which order would you put them in? I dare say that you would put God first, and you would be right. In fact, Satan is not like God or indeed anything like God.

Those of us brought up with the Western worldview have learned to divide reality into what might be called 'the natural' and 'the supernatural', with God and Satan being part of 'the supernatural'. We might therefore be tempted to see them as equal and opposite beings. The Bible, however, divides reality differently. It makes the primary distinction between 'the Creator' and 'the created' (see John 1:3). Like us, Satan is a *created* being whereas God is *the Creator*. There is no comparison. They are not equal and opposite powers or anything remotely like that. Someone once said that to compare Satan to God is like comparing an ant to an atomic bomb. There is no chance whatsoever that Satan could ultimately defeat God.

Jesus came to destroy all of Satan's works. Colossians 2:15 says: 'And having disarmed the powers and authorities, he made a public spectacle of them, triumphing over them by the cross.' At the cross, Jesus completely disarmed Satan. Christ's crucifixion, resurrection and ascension ensure that all authority on earth as well as heaven (not just some!) has been given to him. Jesus is now seated at the right hand of the Father, a symbolic expression that denotes the ultimate seat of power and authority in this universe and all others. He is 'far above' – not just slightly above – all powers and authorities (Ephesians 1:21), words used to describe satanic forces. Starting with the cross, Satan's works are being destroyed. One day they will have been completely destroyed.

In fact, Satan is completely under God's control (see Jude 1:6). Like a dog on a chain, he can only operate within boundaries that God sets. I have two dogs. Our neighbours have a black cat. If the cat ventures into our garden and the dogs see him, they chase him and he turns tail and runs. However, if we take the dogs out for a walk, the cat seems to realize that they are on leads and can only go so far. Often he will come right up to them and parade past slowly just out of reach. Of course, they go wild, snarling, barking and straining at their leads. But the cat knows that he is perfectly safe and seems to amuse himself hugely by standing just a few centimetres beyond the limit of their leads, the picture of calm and tranquillity while they bark themselves hoarse. It's important to know that Satan cannot inflict damage and destruction at will. God lays down very clear boundaries and he simply cannot operate outside of those boundaries.

The big question in terms of spiritual power is where *you* stand in the ranking! God is first but who is next? Are you above or below Satan in terms of your spiritual power?

A young lady approached me after a conference saying that every night for years she had been woken by a scary presence in her bedroom that she knew was demonic. She was in her mid twenties, had moved into a flat of her own but at that point was living back with her parents because the only way she got through the night was actually to get into bed with them.

I showed her a crucial verse: 'Submit to God. Resist the devil and he will flee from you' (James 4:7). I explained to her that she had the power, authority and responsibility to do that. I shared with her how I have taught my own daughters from an early age, if they sense similar spiritual attack, to say something like, 'I give myself to Jesus and I tell the devil to go away', and I suggested that she should do the same. 'I couldn't. I'm not strong enough,' was her response. I explained that Jesus is seated at the right hand of the Father. She knew that. However, what she did *not* know was this verse: 'And God raised us up with Christ and seated us *with* him in the heavenly realms in Christ Jesus' (Ephesians 2:6).

If you are a Christian, you are seated with Christ in that same place of ultimate authority in the heavenly realms, far above all powers and authorities, including Satan himself! Even a two-year-old who has been a Christian just two minutes has that same power and authority. It has nothing to do with maturity or understanding. It is based simply on our position in Christ. The young lady went away from the conference looking quite fearful and doubtful. I didn't have much expectation when she left me that she would act on my advice. I was delighted when she came bounding up to me the next day saying, 'Guess what. It worked!'

She had simply learned that the power and authority she had in Christ was much greater than she had imagined and had taken responsibility to act in faith. It worked. Acting in accordance with the way God says the world is always does!

Satan has a good deal less power that he would have you believe. He would love you to believe, for example, that, like God, he is all-knowing. He is not. It's interesting to note that just about every occult practice has something to do with revealing some 'secret' of the mind or the future. He is trying to fool you into thinking that he knows what you are thinking and what is going to happen. But he does not.

How can I be so sure? Well, for a start Satan is just a created being and does not possess the attributes of God. Why would you think that he would have the power to know the future beyond what God has chosen to reveal or the power to read your thoughts?

There is an interesting story in Daniel 2 that backs this up. King Nebuchadnezzar had had some dreams and he demanded that his sorcerers interpret them. They readily agreed but, in order to be sure of their supernatural credentials, he refused to tell them what was in the dreams. Instead he demanded that they worked that out for themselves. They could not do it because their normal sources of power and information (demons) were presumably unable to read the king's mind. If Satan had been able to read the king's mind, he would surely have passed this information on to the sorcerers and thus prevented Daniel's rise through the ranks.

Now that does not mean that Satan cannot put thoughts *into* your mind, something that the Bible clearly teaches he can do. But so can I. In fact, I hope that I have been doing that through writing the words of this book. If we met face to face I could do it more directly. When communicating this point at a conference, I will often pause and give a huge yawn and then look around... Without fail I see some yawning right back at me. I have succeeded in introducing a thought to their minds!

But just because I can introduce a thought into your mind, does not mean that I can enter it at will and know what is going on in there. I can, however, sometimes make an educated guess. For example, when I am standing up speaking at a conference or a church, I can generally tell who is taking it in and who has their mind on other things just by observing facial expressions and body language – I may not be right 100 per cent of the time but I suspect that I am right most of the time. Similarly, Satan can get a good idea about what may be going on in our minds simply through observation. He's had a lot of practice observing people over many years. He also knows your background. And, of course, it is not hard for him to know what you are thinking if he gave you the thought in the first place!

Some people get spooked because they know someone who went to a medium or some other occult practitioner and was told a detail of their life that no other person – or often only a deceased person – knew. Undoubtedly much of that is explainable through psychology or mind games. However, it would be equally possible that the information was revealed to the medium by a demon which had observed twenty years ago that Great Uncle Bill had a heart-shaped mole on his left buttock.

Many claim that they can see into the future using occult (i.e. satanic) powers. Think about that for a moment. If someone were genuinely able to see into the future, what would they do? I dare say they would make a fortune buying stock-market shares that were about to rise dramatically or betting on rank outsiders in horse races that would then go on to win. What they would not be doing is spending time in tents at funfairs reading palms for £1 a time, advertising for clients on the internet or in the classified section of local newspapers, and selling dubious DVDs promising to change your life. Have you ever seen the headline 'Psychic wins lottery'? Neither have I. I rest my case!

In Isaiah 43:9–12 God makes clear that he is the only one who knows the future (quoted from the New Living Translation):

> Gather the nations together! Assemble the peoples of the world! Which of their idols has ever foretold such things? Which can predict what will happen tomorrow? Where are the witnesses of such predictions? Who can verify that they spoke the truth? 'But you are my witnesses, O Israel!' says the Lord. 'You are my servant. You have been chosen to know me, believe in me, and understand that I alone am God. There is no other God – there never has been, and there never will be. I, yes I, am the Lord, and there is no other Saviour. First I predicted your rescue, then I saved you and proclaimed it to the world. No foreign god has ever done this. You are witnesses that I am the only God,' says the Lord.

Another interesting thing we can deduce from the fact that Satan is simply a created being like you and me is that he can only be in one place at one time. Only God the Creator is everywhere at once. Because Satan operates in the spiritual realms, he can move about freely but he cannot be in two places at once. That means that most of us have probably never come up against Satan himself in person.

If Satan himself can only be in one place at a time, how does he carry on his worldwide rule? Satan works through 'rulers, authorities, powers and spiritual forces of evil in the heavenly realms' (Ephesians 6:12). These terms would have been clearly understood by the original readers of the letter to the Ephesians to apply to different types or levels of spiritual beings. A reasonable assumption would be that he rules through a hierarchy of fallen angels (usually referred to as 'evil spirits' or 'demons'), probably arranged geographically. In fact, the Bible does not tell us very much about exactly how they operate. We can assume that, if we needed to know more, it would tell us.

When I use terms like 'the devil' or 'Satan', then, I am generally using them somewhat generically to mean 'an evil spirit' or 'evil spirits in general'. Satan himself is real enough, of course, but most of us have probably never come up against him in person, though we come up against his minions all the time.

It's time to look at the tactics they use against us.

Tactic 1: Introduce false ideas to deceive us

The Spirit clearly says that in later times some will abandon the faith and follow deceiving spirits and things taught by demons.   (1 TIMOTHY 4:1)

Satan's agenda is to get us to abandon faith and accept false ideas. In the first book in this series we said that faith is simply finding out how things are and living accordingly. Satan wants us to abandon that stance by getting us to believe things that are not true and living accordingly. Paul tells us here that some Christians will fall for it. Of course, if they knew that they were following 'things taught by demons', they would be horrified. But Satan is good at disguising himself – sometimes even as an 'angel of light' (2 Corinthians 11:14) – and his whole aim is to get us to believe a lie without realizing the source of that lie.

Another of Sun Tzu's pearls of wisdom is: 'All warfare is based on deception.' How does Satan deceive us? Well, the battle is for our minds. Neil Anderson has helpfully identified three biblical examples which show how Satan is able to plant his deceptive thoughts in our minds.

Satan rose up against Israel and incited David to take a census of Israel. (1 CHRONICLES 21:1)

Taking a census is not inherently wrong but in this case it was a clear attempt by the enemy to get David to 'abandon faith' by taking his confidence for coming battles off God and putting it onto his own resources. David is described as a man 'after God's own heart'. If Satan had come along undisguised and said in an evil voice, 'David, why don't you sacrifice some babies to me?' David would have dismissed it out of hand. He would never have wanted to further Satan's agenda. In this case too, if he had realized the source of the idea, he would not have done it. The idea of listening to Satan and obeying him would have been repulsive to him. But he did it because he believed that it was his own idea – even though the Bible makes clear that it was not – and that it was a good idea (despite the protestations of the captain of the guard who tried to dissuade him from taking that course of action). Even good people who have a heart for God can be deceived.

The evening meal was being served, and the devil had already prompted Judas Iscariot, son of Simon, to betray Jesus. (JOHN 13:2)

Satan thought that getting Jesus killed would end the threat he posed. Little did he know! Many have debated Judas' motivation for betraying Jesus. He may have thought that it would help move matters on by forcing Jesus to reveal himself as the conquering Messiah. He may simply have been tempted by what he could do with the money he received. Whatever he was thinking, however, I suspect that he had no idea that the thought to do it came from hell itself – but it did. And when Judas realized the implications of what he had done, he was overcome by remorse and went out and hanged himself.

> *Then Peter said, 'Ananias, how is it that Satan has so filled*
> *your heart that you have lied to the Holy Spirit and have kept*
> *for yourself some of the money you received for the land?'*
>
> (ACTS 5:3)

Here we have another example of Satan getting someone to believe a false idea. Ananias fell for the lie that it was outward show that mattered. What had he done? He had sold some land and given most of the money to the church. That's a great thing to do – in most churches he would have been sincerely thanked and honoured. However, he made out that he had given all the money he had received for the land when in fact he had kept some back. He had also fallen for the lie that compromising the truth has no consequences. In fact, God sent a very clear message at that time, through striking him dead, that truth is a crucial issue and cannot be compromised without serious consequences.

So here we have people who were probably for the most part well-meaning but whose actions had awful consequences because they fell for lies fed to them by demons. Satan aims to steal, kill and destroy (John 10:10) and, if he is allowed to, that is exactly what he will do.

How does Satan introduce false ideas to our minds? It is safe to assume that he does not introduce them in a shrieking demonic voice prefaced by cackling laughter, as per the horror films. It must be a lot more subtle than that. In fact, if his aim is to get us to believe that his ideas are our own, it would have to be in a voice that sounds like *our* thoughts. If he is trying to get us to fall for the lie that we are useless, it's a safe bet that the thought will not be '*You* are completely useless, aren't *you*?' but is much more likely to sound exactly like your other thoughts and be along the lines of, '*I* think *I* must be completely useless.'

One of the most important lessons we can learn in this battle for truth that rages in our minds is not to assume that every thought in our head is our own and, therefore, reasonable. Instead we need to hold our thoughts up against the truth in God's Word. Sometimes people ask me, 'How do I know whether a thought is from the enemy or my own?' I think that is to miss the point. The real issue is not where the thought came from but whether or not it is true. And that is something we can ascertain only by comparing it carefully to the truth in the Bible.

Satan works in conjunction with the flesh and the world. He is constantly trying to establish negative flesh patterns in our minds ('I'm no good', 'I'll never be able to'), and to deceive us into worldly ways of thinking ('I can sort this out on my own', 'I'll decide such and such').

This is stating the obvious, I know, but Satan is a really nasty piece of work. Make no mistake about it, if you are a Christian he is out to destroy you. He delights in spoiling that which is good, in desecrating that which is pure and innocent and in killing spiritual life. He has no compassion or sense of fair play.

As I sit down with people and hear about their lives as they go through The Steps To Freedom In Christ, I am often struck by the fact that they seem to have gone through a whole string of experiences that have all given them the same negative message. I recall one man from a good background whom the enemy seemed to have crushed by lining up person after person, experience after experience, to send him the false message that he had no value. His well-meaning father had unwittingly sent him that message, there were teachers who had compounded it, as well as school bullies, and even those who purported to be Christian leaders. The result was that he believed deep down that he was completely without value and, of course, lived accordingly.

I can think of a lady who seemed to go from one relationship to another, and no matter how hard she tried to find 'a good man', ended up being physically abused by her partner.

What was it that led to that same action being repeated again and again? Surely the enemy had a lot to do with it.

If the enemy has enough influence in the minds of others, he can plant thoughts in their minds that they may unwittingly act upon to further his agenda. That provides a salutary warning that he can use us to further his agenda in the lives of others if we let him.

And his agenda is always to deceive us, to get us to abandon faith (seeing reality as it actually is) and to follow the teachings of demons. Those teachings are not always completely untrue, by the way. In fact most of the thoughts and ideas that Satan sends our way start with truth – but end with a lie.

For example, the enemy might remind you of something you have done wrong: 'You looked at that porn site again.' That is true. 'You have let God down and let yourself down.' That is also true. 'There's no way God is going to forgive you this time.' That is not true: 'If we confess our sins, he is faithful and just and will forgive us our sins and purify us from all unrighteousness' (1 John 1:9). Conversely, 'You just led someone to the Lord.' That is true. 'That is a fantastic thing you did. The third this year.' That is true. 'Look at all those other Christians who don't witness. You are a better Christian.' False! Satan is trying to get you into pride. It is God who ultimately does the work as we walk in obedience.

Common areas of deception for the Christian would include thoughts like: 'This might work for others, but my case is different and it won't work for me'; 'I could never have faith like so and so'; or 'God could never use me'. It may be that the circumstances and events that led you to those conclusions were real enough, but the conclusions you have been led to draw are false.

How are you doing in this battle for your mind? Are you deceived? That, of course, is an impossible question to answer. How would you know? By definition, if you are being deceived you don't know it. The deception feels true to you. That is why this is Satan's number-one strategy. I used to think that I had got things pretty much sorted out in my mind. Now I realize that I am likely to spend the rest of my life uncovering deception and constantly realigning my belief system to the truth in God's Word.

Tactic 2: Getting footholds in our lives through sin

Twice in the New Testament Satan is called 'the tempter'. It may appear to us that the tempter is the opposite sex, the bar of chocolate or the unexpected opportunity to make a fast buck. No, those are just the means that Satan uses.

It is important to understand why Satan tempts us. Why is he so keen to get us into sin? Ephesians 4:26–27 gives us a clue:

> 'In your anger do not sin': Do not let the sun go down while you are still angry, and do not give the devil a foothold.

Anger itself is not sinful – it's just an emotion – but if we don't deal with it in short order, it turns to bitterness and unforgiveness, which are sins. The result of falling into sin is that we give the devil a 'foothold'. That word 'foothold' is *topos* in Greek and literally means a 'place'. It's the same word Jesus used when he said he was going to prepare a 'place' for us (John 14:2).

If Satan can lead us into sin, he can gain a 'place', a point of influence in our lives. In terms of the battle for the mind, he gains some influence in our thinking. I have become aware of this in my own life. I have noticed that if I have unconfessed sin in my life, it is as if I leave the enemy a door open to influence my thinking. He does not take advantage of this until it is in his interests to do so – for example, when I am about to move on with the Lord or am in a situation where others are doing business with God, perhaps in a small group at church.

I have noticed that I will suddenly get a thought that seems to me to be really witty, and I feel an almost irresistible urge to share it. When I do, others do generally find it funny, but often I have simply served to defuse something that the Lord was doing and have caused it to degenerate into triviality. That is not to say that there is no place for jokes and funny stories in the Christian life! It's just that in my case the enemy often wants to use them to deflect people away from what God is doing. Sometimes I have watched lovely Christians suddenly go red in the face in a church meeting, leap to their feet and yell or storm out, slamming the door behind them. Usually they are simply not the sort of people who would do that. What's happening? I would hazard a guess that the enemy is taking advantage of a 'place' in their mind and influencing their thinking so that again they become a distraction from what God is doing.

There is another passage that sheds some light on this: 'If you forgive anyone, I also forgive him. And what I have forgiven – if there was anything to forgive – I have forgiven in the sight of Christ for your sake, in order that Satan might not outwit us. For we are not unaware of his schemes' (2 Corinthians 2:10–11).

The more usual way to translate the Greek word here rendered 'schemes' would be 'thoughts'. That's a very interesting fact when it comes to the battle we are facing for our minds – 'we are not unaware of his thoughts'. In this case, Paul implies that if we are not aware of the thoughts Satan puts into our minds (or, if you prefer, the schemes he tends to use against us), he will outwit us. In my experience the sin of unforgiveness is holding more Christians back than anything else, and they are blissfully unaware that it is a trap of the enemy. We will look at it in some detail in the next book in the series. Even though there is no reason whatsoever why we should be outwitted by Satan, we can allow it to happen.

The Lord gave me a graphic illustration of how these footholds of the enemy function in our lives. I was returning with my family from a holiday in Spain. The flight we were booked on was running late and everyone was tired. It was with a budget airline that did not allocate seat numbers and, at this particular airport, they made no attempt to board passengers in an orderly fashion, so it was something of a free-for-all. As soon as it looked as if the flight might be ready, a queue formed and I leapt forward – I was proud to get myself into eighth place (though I had no idea where the rest of the family were!).

I boarded the plane and headed for a block of seats in front of the wing. However, as I walked down the aisle I became aware that it was getting more and more difficult to move forwards. I was focused on getting the seats I wanted, so I simply dismissed those thoughts from my mind and carried on. However, I eventually came to a point where it was impossible to take another step and I ground to a halt with a load of impatient people behind me.

It took just a moment to work out what the problem was. I became aware that the toggle on my jacket, which was on an elastic cord, had got caught on the first row of seats – I was now at row eleven! I couldn't move forward until someone released it for me. As it happened, my wife was coming onto the plane at that time and she was the one who released the toggle, which came hurtling down the plane, much to the amusement of my fellow passengers!

That's exactly how it is, if you have unresolved personal and spiritual conflicts or, in other words, footholds of the enemy. You can try to move forwards, to grow as a Christian as much as you like. But it won't happen. You will grind to a halt.

This was brought home to me when I was trying to disciple a couple in my church. They really wanted to move on and, in their words, 'be like everyone else'. I realized that the issue for their freedom was getting them to know the truth, so I determined to get the simplest, most straightforward teaching

I could find, and we met once a week to go through it. That, of course, is a straight reflection of the Western worldview – if someone doesn't know the truth, tell them; if they still don't get it, tell them again!

I remember one week they wrestled with the concept that God just loved them, no matter what they had done. By the end of the evening it seemed that they had finally got it. However, the following week when we were looking at some other topic, they said, 'But we don't feel God loves us.' To be honest with you, I wanted to pin them up against the wall by their collars and growl at them, 'We did that last week!'

I soon realized that this lovely couple were simply not going to make any progress with me just *telling* them the truth. They needed to know the truth in order to be set free, but my just telling them the truth was not working. I've since realized that I am just the same. No matter how many excellent sermons I listen to or wonderful books I read, if I don't also deal with the footholds of the enemy in my life, I will not 'get it'. This couple were the first people I ever took through the Steps To Freedom. The effects were instant and dramatic. Just clearing away some footholds of the enemy enabled them immediately to get hold of the truth that previously had seemed so elusive.

The great majority of Christians have been taught the truth very well for years. But they still don't get it. Why not? Because they haven't known how to close the open doors that enable the enemy to influence their thinking. For example, if you have never truly forgiven someone who hurt you, you are leaving a big door open to the enemy to confuse your thinking and stop you connecting with truth. If you do not close that door by obeying God and forgiving that person, no matter how well someone preaches the truth to you, you are unlikely ever really to get hold of it in a way that you can grasp and put into practice.

It's very important to stress at this point that we're not talking about Christians being 'possessed' – that is, completely taken over or taken back by demons. At the centre of your being, your spirit is connected to God's Spirit, and Satan can't have you back. You have been bought by the blood of Jesus (1 Peter 1:18–19). In other words, this is not about ownership (or 'possession'). In fact, the word 'possession' is not a biblical term in this context. It was introduced into the English language via the King James version of the Bible. In the original text, in most cases the term used is simply that someone 'had' a demon. In other cases, a word is used that is literally translated as 'demonized'. English translations tend to render these as 'demon-possessed', which unfortunately implies ownership, or at least that the people concerned were helpless to do anything about it. In fact, that is not the case – even the man who said he had a 'legion' of demons was able to choose to come to Jesus to be set free. The conclusion we can come to is that Christians can never be owned by Satan but can unwittingly allow him to have different levels of influence (or footholds) in their mind.

We read in 2 Corinthians 4:4 that Satan 'has blinded the minds of unbelievers', and the effect of these footholds seems to work in believers in much the same way. They cause a degree of spiritual blindness and make it more difficult for us to 'connect' with truth.

The good news is that these footholds can be overcome in Christ through repenting and resisting the enemy. The Steps To Freedom In Christ by Neil Anderson is a tool you can use to do this in a gentle and controlled way. You simply ask the Lord to show you, across all areas of your life, where there is unresolved sin that may be giving the enemy a foothold and, when the Lord shows you, you deal with the sin. That takes away the enemy's ability to influence your thinking, and many find that they are then able to get hold of truth in a completely new way. We will look more at this process in the next book in the series.

My own testimony is that going through the Steps to Freedom seemed something of a matter-of-fact, unexciting process. No fireworks went off. There was no great revelation or warm fuzzy feeling. However, over the following weeks I became aware that I was getting so much more out of my daily Bible reading. Up to that point I would read the Bible and think, 'Oh yes, I've read that bit before' and had given up thinking that there was any 'new' truth. From that moment on, I have found that I can get 'stuck' in a passage for days because there seems to be so much in there. All that happened was that by repenting I took away the enemy's ability to blind me to truth.

In the Western church we have usually been taught to confess our sin but not what it means to repent. As well as turning from sin, complete repentance involves removing the influence we have given to the enemy and then going on to renew our mind.

We will look at how to resist temptation when we come to consider our final enemy, the flesh. As we shall see, when it comes to enticing us into sin, Satan tends to work through the flesh.

Tactic 3: Accusation

In Revelation 12:10, Satan is called 'the accuser' and we read that he accuses Christians day and night. Are you aware of his accusations against you? In fact, you might not think that the sorts of accusations he routinely makes against you are accusations at all. They tend to manifest themselves as thoughts such as 'I'm stupid', 'I'm no good', 'I'll never change', 'God doesn't love me', 'I'm different from others'. None of those things is true, of course, but if he can get us to believe that they are, they will have a negative impact on our behaviour.

His accusation works most effectively when he is able to convince you that it is coming not from him but from God, and particularly in conjunction with tempting thoughts that you have given in to.

I was involved in backing up a church who were helping a young lady caught in various addictions. She really wanted to move on with God. Her addictions were just ways of blotting out the pain caused by trauma in her past, and she was gradually learning to resolve the pain in Christ. However, occasionally she would fall for the temptation to hit the bottle. As soon as she did that, the gentle, tempting voice ('You know you really want to...no one will know... It really will help you...) turned into the voice of the accuser: 'You have failed again. You'll never make it as a Christian.' In fact, it would seem to her as if God himself were telling her that he had written her off – something which, of course, he would never do.

As a young Christian, I found myself particularly susceptible to this sort of accusation. If I fell into sin, it would often take weeks for me to recover because I felt that God was condemning me. In fact, it was simply the accusations of the enemy. If you fall off a bike or a horse, the advice most people will give is to get straight back on it and keep riding. It's like that in the Christian life too. If we fall into some sin, there is nothing to stop us dealing with it immediately by confessing it to God, turning away from it and closing the door we opened to the enemy, then getting straight back on with our walk with the Lord. Satan's accusations are designed to make us feel that we cannot do that, that we cannot approach God, that we are hopeless or unworthy. It's almost as though we're unconsciously punishing ourselves even though Jesus has already taken the punishment and the way to God is open.

Unfortunately, other Christians can unwittingly collude with the enemy in this and join in the accusation and condemnation. When the young lady struggling with addiction fell, she always called me because she knew I would not do that. I would tell her, 'Well, nothing has changed. God still loves you. You know how to deal with this so just do it and get back on your bike.' If she was not reassured of that, the chances were that she would be even more inclined to turn to her addictions again.

Tactic 4: Fear

Even though he is defeated, Satan still 'prowls around, like a roaring lion looking for someone to devour' (1 Peter 5:8). He loves to inspire fear in us because that is the closest he will get to worship.

The reality, of course, is that we have no reason whatsoever to fear Satan or demons. As we have already seen, Jesus came to destroy the works of Satan (1 John 3:8). He defeated Satan at the cross and disarmed him (Colossians 2:15). Christ's crucifixion, resurrection and ascension ensure that all authority on earth as well as in heaven has been given to him, and we share that because of our position in him at God's right hand, 'far above all rule and authority, power and dominion' (Ephesians 1:21).

There is nothing big about a demon except its mouth! They are like dogs with a big bark but no teeth. We do not need to be intimidated by some little thing that goes bump in the night. It should be the other way round. Demons are petrified of Christians who know the extent of the power and authority they have in Christ.

One of my daughters' friends is frightened of dogs. Despite the fact that our dogs are nice and friendly, when she comes round to play they have to be kept in a separate room. But guess what always happens... Someone opens the door and they get out. When she sees them, what does she do? She leaps up onto the nearest piece of furniture. She's quite a big girl and the dogs are quite small. Now, what power do those dogs have to get her up onto the dining-room table? Only what she gave them. How did she get up there? The dogs used her mind, her emotions, her will and her muscles. What would have happened if she had stood her ground? They would have licked her a little, lost interest and gone away. In the same way, demons have no power over Christians except what we give them.

The difficulty we have with this whole subject comes back in large measure to the worldview issue. In the West we have simply not been brought up to be aware of the spiritual world. Even if we have acknowledged its existence, we have put it into 'the supernatural realm' which, we have been taught, has nothing to do with daily life. And, of course, if we think about the fact that there are malevolent spiritual beings who want to mess our lives up, that is a scary thought. Some might say, 'Do you mean there might be demons targeting me right now?' Yes, the spiritual world is filled with demons, but so what? You have no reason to be frightened about that. If we fix our eyes on Jesus and live a righteous life by faith in the power of the Holy Spirit, there is nothing they can do to stop us. We are the ones with all the power and the authority – not them!

The real danger comes for those Christians who don't realize that the demons are there or who don't understand the way they work and how to protect themselves. When doctors didn't know about microbes, they didn't sterilize their instruments or scrub their hands, and people died. Christians who don't know about the reality of the spiritual world don't see any need to put on the armour of God and 'take captive every thought to make it obedient to Christ' (2 Corinthians 10:5). That makes it easy for the enemy to neutralize them. People become casualties. Some 'shipwreck their faith' (see 1 Timothy 1:19).

I first began to understand the demonic when I read *The Bondage Breaker* by Neil Anderson. Shortly after that I came across another book by Neil called *Spiritual Protection For Your Children* and took it with me as holiday reading for our annual two-week family holiday in France. At this point I had no idea that I would become involved with Freedom In Christ Ministries – but perhaps the enemy did. The book told the story of a family's struggles with demonic activity and, being brought up with the Western worldview, I found it interesting but somewhat out of my experience. I also found it a little unnerving to realize that demons were real and targeted Christians. Perhaps you have felt much the same as you have read this chapter. Anyway, one night my elder daughter, then aged seven, came into our bedroom and said that she had had a bad dream. I asked her what it was about but she didn't want to say. I persuaded her to tell me: 'There were lots of people in hoods and they killed you and Mummy.' Well, we prayed together and committed it to the Lord, and she went back to bed. Now that was an unusual dream for her to have on many levels. She was not prone to nightmares and she had never seen any horror films – wherever could such an image have come from? I found it a little unnerving but after some more praying went back to sleep, only to be woken up a little later by my younger daughter, age five. She said that she was having nightmares. Guess what they were about? Exactly the same thing as my other daughter! She used practically the same words to describe it. Was I scared? You bet! We were staying in an old farm building that, in any case, felt dark and creepy, and now this was happening. I didn't get much sleep the rest of the night but spent most of it praying.

That incident could easily have made me decide that I didn't want anything to do with the demonic or any ministry dealing with it. After all, maybe it would put my family at risk. Thankfully, the Lord simply showed me that all Satan can do is try to scare us. If we use the armour and weapons at our disposal, he cannot touch us. A decade on, and I can testify to the Lord's faithfulness in keeping my family absolutely safe as we have followed what he has given us to do. If Satan could have harmed us or stopped us, he would have done. The truth is, he has not been able to. In fact, as we have previously noted, none of us has a choice to opt out of the battle. We are in it. It is raging all around us. Our only choice is to engage in it and protect ourselves or to ignore it and become a casualty.

The enemy will attack us wherever he can find legitimate grounds. In my experience, this often happens when I am staying away from home, something I get to do reasonably frequently. I find, however, that simply having a basic understanding of the way the spiritual world works and of my power and authority in Christ, enables me to prevent the enemy attacking even before he has begun. Before I leave home for a trip I will make a declaration along the lines of, 'I declare that I am head of this household and I commit it to Jesus while I am away. I forbid the enemy from interfering with or attacking my family or any part of my domain while I am away.' In the same way, when I arrive at where I am staying, I will make a similar declaration, something like, 'I declare that I am staying in this room by legal right. If anything has gone on in this room that has been sinful and given the enemy any ground, I take it away now by covering it with the blood of Jesus, and I command the enemy to leave and stay away.' That makes for a good night's sleep.

Given that 50 per cent of hotel guests use pay-per-view porn, you can guarantee that the enemy has been given ground in practically any hotel you stay in. It makes sense to take that ground away. It's no big deal. It doesn't take very long. But it makes a real difference. I don't do these things in any kind of superstitious way. It would not be a disaster if I forgot – if I sensed the enemy attacking, that would cause me to remember and I would do it then. This is just a matter of realizing what reality is like and living accordingly, in much the same way as I would take the precaution of turning the electricity off at the mains if I were going to do any electrical work at home. If I had known how to make a similar declaration at the time we were on holiday in France, my daughters would not have been troubled by those nightmares.

Tactic 5: Making us think that people are the enemy

Have you ever seen demonic activity in your church? How would you recognize it if it occurred? Perhaps you are thinking that it would be seen in 'dramatic' episodes of people rolling around on the floor and screaming or disrupting meetings. Those things certainly can be demonic, but they are few and far between, and that serves to reinforce the false idea that we don't come up against demons very much in the West.

In fact, as we have seen, the battle is primarily in the mind of every Christian. If we allow the enemy to keep the footholds we have given him through sin, we risk allowing him to use us to further his agenda, and that agenda is the direct opposite of God's purpose for the church.

What would you say is God's purpose for the church? In the context of talking about his own ministry of preaching the good news to non-Jews, Paul says it is this: 'His intent was that now, through the church, the manifold wisdom of God should be made known to the rulers and authorities in the heavenly realms, according to his eternal purpose which he accomplished in Christ Jesus our Lord' (Ephesians 3:10). Those 'rulers and authorities', of course, are demons. Our whole purpose is to be a living demonstration to Satan of God's incredible wisdom. As sinful people turn to Christ and are transformed, then go out and show his love and compassion, there is a powerful demonstration of God's wisdom. Jesus gave the church a commission along similar lines, conferring on us his power and authority and saying, 'Go and make disciples of all nations, baptizing them in the name of the Father and of the Son and of the Holy Spirit, and teaching them to obey everything I have commanded you' (Matthew 28:19–20).

What is the main thing preventing people out there from becoming part of the church, from turning to Christ and being transformed? Paul says clearly it is because the enemy has 'blinded the minds of unbelievers' (2 Corinthians 4:4). Nonbelievers too face a battle for their minds. They simply cannot see the truth of the good news of Christ, no matter how clearly it is presented to them, because the enemy is causing spiritual blindness.

In the light of all that, if you could ask God for one thing to enable the church to fulfil its commission, so that people out there will believe in Jesus, what would you ask for? Interestingly, we have recorded in the Bible one thing that Jesus prayed specifically for Christians who would come after the disciples – in other words, for us. He could have prayed any number of things but he chose this. He asked (in John 17:21) that, 'all of them may be one, Father, just as you are in me and I am in you. May they also be in us so that the world may believe that you have sent me.'

Seeing people become Christians and the church being united may not at first glance seem to be closely related. However, note that Jesus also said that it was because of our love for each other that people would know that we are his disciples. When we love each other, we are demonstrating the truth that we are one. And something significant happens spiritually when we are one:

> How good and pleasant it is when brothers live together in unity! It is like precious oil poured on the head, running down on the beard, running down on Aaron's beard, down upon the collar of his robes. It is as if the dew of Hermon were falling on Mount Zion. For there the Lord commands his blessing, even life for evermore. (PSALM 133:1–3)

Unity has a spiritual effect. It causes God to command a blessing. Disunity brings about the opposite. The New Testament is littered with exhortations to Christians such as this one: 'I appeal to you, brothers, in the name of our Lord Jesus Christ, that all of you agree with one another so that there may be no divisions among you and that you may be perfectly united in mind and thought' (1 Corinthians 1:10).

Have you ever wondered why it is that the early church – which had no resources and faced a very difficult spiritual environment and lots of opposition – was able to see thousands of people becoming Christians in just one day? Could this be the answer: 'All the believers were one in heart and mind' (Acts 4:32)? If they were perfectly united, they were unstoppable. Satan appeared unable to keep people in spiritual blindness.

Satan's agenda for the church, being the direct opposite of God's purpose for it, is to cause disunity so that there is no blessing and people remain in spiritual blindness. That is why so much of the enemy's activity is directed at causing division.

If you want to see demonic activity in your church, look for it in people falling out with each other, criticism (particularly of leaders), backbiting and unforgiveness. The enemy concentrates on trying to make us fall out with each other, emphasize our differences, and put truth above grace.

But when we see those things happening, surely it's the people themselves who are to blame, isn't it? Well, they certainly cannot be absolved from responsibility, but that is not the whole story. The classic passage on spiritual warfare is Ephesians 6:10–20, about the armour God has given us to resist Satan's attacks. In it, Paul says, 'For our struggle is not against flesh and blood, but against the rulers, against the authorities, against the powers of this dark world and against the spiritual forces of evil in the heavenly realms. Therefore put on the full armour of God...'

If we don't realize who our enemy really is, we fall for the lie that we are fighting flesh-and-blood people and we end up hitting out at each other. People do have a responsibility not to let the enemy use them but, even if they do, they are not the enemy – Satan is.

This has been brought home to me clearly as I have had the privilege of helping church leadership teams go through a 'Setting Your Church Free' process where they identify footholds of the enemy in the corporate structure of their church and kick them out. Usually, when it is perceived that there are problems in a church, individuals are held responsible. Indeed, they do hold some responsibility, but if we concentrate solely on that, we can miss the bigger picture of what is going on behind the scenes. It may well be that individuals have left enough doors open to the enemy's influence in their minds that he is able to 'press their buttons' and influence them into doing things that are not helpful, but make no mistake – the enemy is mixed up in it.

I can think of one occasion where the leadership team contained two members who were from families that had always been in the church and had a history of control. These two men were blamed for a lot of the problems in the church. As the leaders went through the process, they all agreed together (including the two men concerned) that control was an issue in the church and renounced it. As soon as the process was over, the leadership team noticed a distinct change in the spiritual atmosphere in the church. Astonishingly, in the next couple of weeks these two leaders who, it was thought, would never relinquish control, decided independently and freely to step down from their leadership positions. They became fruitful members of the church. In other words, they really were not the problem. They were influenced by it and may well have gone along with it when they could have chosen not to, but the real problem was a spiritual one. The team was not fighting flesh and blood but the spiritual forces of evil in the heavenly realms. For years they had been battling each other. Just one simple 'arrow' directed at the real cause of the problem fixed it immediately.

That prickly person in your church who is always criticizing you is not your enemy. Neither is the pastor who didn't understand you; or the small-group leader who didn't know how to help you and seemed to ignore you. No Christian, no matter what they have done, is your enemy. Instead we are all part of the body of Christ and, for the sake of those who do not yet know him, we must be united. It takes two to cause division. That is not, of course, to absolve people of their responsibility. 'The devil made me do it' is a deception – no one has to go along with his agenda.

This is the verse that speaks most to me about keeping the unity of the Spirit in the church: 'If it is possible, as far as it depends on you, live at peace with everyone' (Romans 12:18). It is the 'as far as it depends on you' bit that I find most helpful. We will return to this theme and look practically at how we can live in genuine unity in the fourth book in this series.

Our Defence Against the Devil

Understand how the battle works

In the West our worldview predisposes us against seeing the reality of the spiritual world. We therefore have some work to do in simply understanding how it works. It's not that complicated and we have laid out the basics. If you were to ask me to sum it up, I would say this: Yes, Satan and his demons are as real as your next-door neighbour and they are out to get you. However, you hold all the cards and if you use the defences God has given you, you can get on with your life without any fear or trepidation because you are seated with Christ in the ultimate seat of power and authority.

Remove every foothold of the enemy

Again because of our predisposition not to take the spiritual world seriously, we have not generally understood the serious consequences of our sin giving the enemy a foothold, a base of operations in our mind from which he can influence our thinking. It's very straightforward to remove these footholds but we have generally not been taught how to do it, and consequently we have left many of them in place.

We have been taught to say sorry to God for our sins as if the only thing that was of consequence was the offence we caused to him. It is, of course, right to do that. That is what the Bible calls confession. But simply confessing our sins does not remove the foothold. As we have said, we also need to submit to God through repentance and resist the devil (see James 4:7).

Fill our minds with truth

Our minds are the battleground, so it stands to reason that we need to guard them, taking care to allow into them only what is helpful. If we spend a lot of our time watching TV programmes with sexual content, it will not come as a great surprise when we are plagued by lustful thoughts.

If you are already in that position and want to change, how do you do it? Concentrating on not thinking lustful thoughts is not effective. Trying not to think negative thoughts doesn't work. I remember once being stuck in a traffic jam on a motorway, absolutely desperate to go to relieve myself. Telling myself not to think about it only made it worse. It was impossible to do that. The answer was actually to force myself to think about something else entirely. In the same way, instead of concentrating on not having lustful thoughts – which does not work – the answer is to think of something pure. Here is the best advice I know:

> Finally, brothers, whatever is true, whatever is noble, whatever is right, whatever is pure, whatever is lovely, whatever is admirable – if anything is excellent or praiseworthy – think about such things.   (PHILIPPIANS 4:8)

We fill our minds with truth which gradually replaces the negative things we have allowed in.

Deceiving spirits also have more subtle ways of gaining access to our minds. In particular, we need to be on our guard for anything that would persuade us to put our minds into neutral, as Eastern religions and New Age thinking urge us to do, because we may unwittingly allow the enemy to take advantage of that passive state. It is not at all uncommon nowadays for meditation techniques involving 'emptying' our mind to be taught in business training and in schools. I've even known it sneak into churches.

The Bible, however, never tells us to direct our thoughts inwardly or passively but always outwardly and actively. It is good to invite God to 'Search me, O God, and know my heart; test me and know my anxious thoughts' (Psalm 139:23), but God always works through our mind.

We are transformed by the renewing of our minds (Romans 12:2). In his definitive teaching on tongues and prophecy Paul says, 'I will pray with my spirit, but I will also pray with my mind; I will sing with my spirit, but I will also sing with my mind' (1 Corinthians 14:15). Our minds are always involved when God works.

The enemy loves to masquerade as God and to counterfeit everything that God does. Counterfeit spiritual gifts usually come about by some passive state of the mind when the person is almost in a trance like that of a medium. If someone is using a legitimate gift of tongues, their mind is fully engaged, aware of what is going on around them. God does not bypass their mind.

Some have been taught that Christians who are 'really spiritual' should hear God's voice all the time. In my experience this too can open us up to deceiving spirits. I came across a student who was desperate to hear God's voice about everything – he ended up feeling guilty if he did not hear a voice from the Lord, or confused when following a thought he believed had come from God did not turn out well. Not every voice in our mind claiming to be God or sounding like God actually is. My advice to him was to stop straining to hear God's voice every day and simply get on with living a righteous life in the power of the Holy Spirit, confident that God would lead and guide as necessary.

I remember once in my own experience, at a time when the Lord was clearly leading us as a ministry to pray for a particular building, having a thought come into my head telling me to go urgently to the building and pray. I stopped my car and started to turn it around – but something did not feel right. This voice was insistent and urgent, almost hectoring. Was it really the Lord? Yet on the other hand, would a demon really be telling me to go and pray about something that was clearly in line with God's will? I stopped the car and considered. I came to the conclusion that this was not God but a demon trying to 'gain my confidence' by giving me an apparently good thing to do. I have since come across people who thought they were hearing God's voice but gradually the things that 'God' told them to do became more and more bizarre. By that time, however, they were hooked and had a hard time giving up their 'special voice'.

Don't misunderstand me. We can, of course, expect God to speak to us and to give us clear guidance. Generally speaking, however, he sets out guidelines, principles and a direction, and leaves us to walk forward by faith. He never seems to be in a hurry but over time gives us consistent promptings through the Holy Spirit and other people to enable us to know his specific direction for us. If we go wrong he tells us: 'Whether you turn to the right or the left your ears will hear a voice behind you saying, "This is the way, walk in it"' (Isaiah 30:21). Note that he calls from behind when we go wrong rather than continuously calling to us from in front.

Over time we develop discernment as Christians, a sense within of what is right or wrong. God has also given us other Christians around us whom we can bounce things off to see what they discern. Those who refuse to submit themselves to the counsel of other mature Christians are much more likely to pay attention to a deceiving spirit, believing that they are hearing the voice of God.

Although we need to be very aware of the enemy and guard our minds from his attacks, the answer is not to pay undue attention to him but to concentrate on truth. I came across a lady who was so serious about guarding her mind that she would literally spend hours every day rebuking the enemy ('I rebuke that thought... And I rebuke that thought too...'). Should we keep checking our thoughts and rebuking the enemy every five minutes to see if he has put a thought into our mind?

Getting too hung up on the thoughts themselves is akin to

getting a load of spam e-mails and sitting down and replying to them all:

> Thank you so much for your concern about my sexual prowess. I am pleased to tell you, however, that there is no need for you to worry about that on my account. So I would be grateful if you would not send me any more e-mails of this variety. I do, however, appreciate your concern. Please pass on my regards to your wife who, I trust, is benefiting from your astonishing range of products. Yours sincerely...

That, of course, would be time-consuming and would accomplish nothing apart from indicating to the spammer that your e-mail address is active, which would lead to more spam. What's the answer? As soon as you see that a message is spam, simply delete it and get on with life. When it comes to thoughts that are not in line with truth, simply ignore them and get on with life. Choose the truth.

Others get hung up about whether a particular thought is from the enemy. It's good that they are taking the whole thing seriously but in both cases they are becoming demon-focused rather than Christ-focused. As we noted previously, the question to ask is not so much what the source of the thought is but whether or not it is true. Satan has no power over us at all unless he can deceive us into believing that he does – and we only give him that power when we fail to believe the truth.

Do you know how bank workers are trained to recognize counterfeit currency? By studying carefully various samples of counterfeits? No! By studying over and over again the real thing. They become so intimately acquainted with what genuine notes are like that they are able to spot fakes when they come along. In the same way, our defence against deception is to acquaint ourselves intimately with truth.

This battle for our minds revolves around truth. The answer is always to expose Satan's lie to God's truth, to bring it into the light – and immediately his power is broken. His lies cannot withstand the truth any more than the darkness of night can withstand the rising sun. This is not a question of who has more power – you do. It's a question of truth and lies.

As we immerse ourselves in truth (i.e. commit ourselves to the biblical worldview) and become more and more acquainted with it, it will become increasingly difficult for the enemy to influence us with his deception because we will spot it as soon as it enters our mind.

Don't let Satan set the agenda

In my early days of helping people using this approach, I came out of my church to see a man standing at the other side of the car park making odd movements with his hands towards the church. He looked as if he was saying something too. As soon as he saw me, he jumped into the passenger seat of a car that was waiting with its engine running, which immediately screeched off down the road exactly like a getaway car in an armed robbery. It was fairly clear to me that he had been pronouncing some kind of curse against the church. Should I have been concerned about that? Not especially.

A curse is simply like a prayer, except that it's directed to the enemy. In effect the man was asking the enemy to target an evil spirit at our ministry. However, we are the ones seated with Christ at the right hand of the Father, far above all demonic beings. We are the ones with the real power and authority – witness the fact that the man concerned fled as soon as he saw me. Also, to be honest, if evil spirits aren't already targeting me and my ministry, I would want to ask myself why not! If a similar thing happened again, I would simply say something like, 'I break that curse in the name of Jesus and I ask you, Lord Jesus, to bless that guy and save him', and leave it at that.

That is not to say that we don't need to take curses spoken

against us seriously. Proverbs 26:2 says, 'Like a fluttering sparrow or a darting swallow, an undeserved curse does not come to rest.' We can infer that, when a curse is deserved because of some sinful action we have taken, it may 'come to rest'. This would be the same thing as giving the devil a foothold, a point of influence in our lives. If, however, we are careful to keep short accounts with the Lord and deal with any foothold we give the enemy by repenting and resisting, then it doesn't matter how many people curse us, that curse will not 'come to rest'.

The other way a curse might hurt us is if we (wrongly) believe that it can. In that case they tend to become like self-fulfilling prophecies or any other lie that we believe that is not in line with God's truth. People who have been brought up in an animistic culture (for example, in Africa) or those who tend to overemphasize the power of the enemy, are particularly vulnerable to this. They can get caught in the trap of thinking that there must be some 'key' as to why they are not living a fruitful life in Christ and conclude that it must be down to a curse. In fact, the truth is that they already have everything they need to live a godly life (2 Peter 1:3) and have been blessed with every spiritual blessing in the heavenly realms (Ephesians 1:3). If they are not connecting with that, the answer is simply repentance and faith (believing the truth).

I sometimes get Christians who are keen to alert me to dates of occult festivals and other such things. They are surprised when I don't take a great deal of interest. C. S. Lewis astutely pointed out that Satan is pleased if we act as if he does not exist at all but equally pleased if we go to the other extreme and develop an unhealthy interest in him. Of course, the activities of Satanists are harmful to themselves and potentially to others. However, when it comes to spiritual power, we have far more than they do. If we are not careful, we will find ourselves acting as if it is the other way around, as if we are the ones who need to be frightened. And that is exactly how Satan likes it.

I'm not that impressed either when people tell me – as they often do – that the place where they live is particularly 'dark'. I'm not doubting what they say. But the whole world is in the power of the evil one and it's difficult to imagine that where they live is any darker than the occult world faced by the early church, and they simply went out there and made disciples in their thousands. We need to see through the enemy's intention to scare us off and get on with the job. If it's a dark place, let's use what God has given us and make it lighter!

You will note that I have not talked about 'casting out' a demon. Jesus and Paul both cast demons out of other people in the sense that they came with superior spiritual power and forced the demon to leave. However, in all those cases, the people concerned were not Christians. If a non-Christian suddenly came at me with a knife and I sensed there was a demon behind it, I would have no hesitation in doing the same thing.

When it comes to Christians, however, it is a different matter. There are no instructions in the Bible for casting a demon out of another Christian. Instead there is a clear instruction to individual Christians about what to do if the enemy is an issue: 'Submit to God. Resist the devil and he will flee from you' (James 4:7). Who has to do the submitting and resisting? The individual Christian. It is not something that you or I are called to do for them.

If a Christian has a spiritual issue and you rightly discern some demonic influence, what is the main problem? The demon? No. The reason the demon is able to operate is because a foothold was given to the enemy through sin. In effect the demon is just a symptom. The main problem is the sin that opened the door and which has not been dealt with. As we have seen, it is straightforward to repent of the sin and resist the enemy. That will resolve the issue. If, however, I succeed in 'casting out' the demon but the sin is not dealt with, that leaves the door wide open for the enemy to return, something in fact that Jesus clearly warned would happen (Luke 11:24–26).

Be aware of Satan's schemes

Paul said, 'we are not unaware of Satan's schemes' (2 Corinthians 2:11). Is that true of you? Are you aware of the ways that he tends to attack you, the particular ways in which you are vulnerable to attack, the truths that you struggle to take hold of and which the enemy ruthlessly preys on? We are all unique people with a unique set of circumstances and a unique set of weaknesses. Satan's schemes against you will be a little different from the ones he uses against me.

Knowing how your enemy attacks you is half the battle. That way you can prepare your defence. I know, for example, that I am particularly vulnerable to condemning thoughts and that is a strategy that the enemy has historically used against me with some success. I now prepare myself for these. For a start, I spend time focusing on the truths of who I am in Christ and understanding that God will never, ever condemn me. I have learned key Bible verses such as Romans 8:1, which says that there is no condemnation for me because I am in Christ. I have noticed that I am particularly vulnerable to these thoughts after I have been involved in a speaking engagement and, when they come, I recognize them for what they are and deal with them accordingly. I remind myself of the truth, I pray, I sometimes thank God out loud that there is no condemnation, that I am a child of his, that his acceptance of me has nothing to do with my behaviour and so on.

I used to have a problem with watching the wrong sort of stuff on TV. That whole area is one that I now treat with a great deal of caution. I have trained myself to look carefully at the content of TV programmes I may watch and not watch those that are not edifying. I have learned to recognize the sort of 'excuse' for ignoring those warning signs that may pop into my mind and dismiss it.

Once you know Satan's schemes, you really can be ready for them. Why not spend some time right now with a blank sheet of paper and a pen asking the Lord to reveal to you what Satan's schemes against you are, in particular what lies you have been prone to believe. Then take some action to prepare yourself for the next time he uses them. Remember that you can lift up the shield of faith which quenches every burning arrow of the evil one (Ephesians 6:16). But that does require some effort, some preparatory work.

Commit yourself to unity

If, as we saw earlier, unity in the church has an effect on whether or not unbelievers come to Christ, it's something that we need to take very seriously indeed. This is particularly important for those who, like us, live in a society that stresses individuality far above corporate responsibility. Criticism and blame-casting are woven into the very fabric of our society, but as Christians we need to recognize them for what they are – schemes of the enemy – and refuse to have anything to do with them.

I can guarantee that if you are in a church you will be tempted to rebel against your leaders, to criticize your fellow Christians, to fall out with them and then remain in unforgiveness. If the enemy can, he will push you towards becoming entrenched in your views so that you are certain that you are right and others are wrong. He will want you to put an emphasis on truth rather than grace so that you will see the imperfections that undoubtedly exist in others but do not balance them with the grace that has been shown to you. He wants to lead you down a path that will end in damaged relationships and, if he can, a church split.

Again, this comes down simply to recognizing Satan's schemes. The answer is to understand what he is up to and ensure that you do the opposite. I remember when I first became aware of all the negative thoughts that came into my head about my pastor. Many of the thoughts were based on truth (something he had done or said in the heat of the moment or simply a mistake he had made) but were designed to get me to the point where I openly gossiped or criticized. I learned to see these for what they were and so simply did the opposite of what they were designed to do. I would pray out loud, 'Lord, thank you so much for my pastor. I pray that you would bless him and encourage him. Give him wisdom…etc. etc.' I felt when I did that, it was almost as if a look of dismay came over the face of a demon who then said, 'Hey, that wasn't meant to happen!' I'd find that the negative thoughts diminished hugely but that they would reappear at some point in the future when the demon thought he'd have another crack at it.

This is not to say, incidentally, that church leaders should go unchallenged if they consistently do things wrong, and the Bible lays out clear guidelines for how you should handle sin in the life of another Christian (we'll look at this in the fourth book in this series). However, I come across Christians all the time who have fallen for these temptations to criticize. They are convinced that their leaders are completely in the wrong and going in the wrong direction. Yet when asked if they can actually name a specific sin that the leader is consistently committing, they cannot. Or, if they can, they have not handled it biblically by going to see the leader and expressing their concern – instead they have told everyone else and played right into the enemy's hands.

As a member of a church I do not always immediately see the logic in what my leaders decide. Sometimes I will share my view with them. However, at the end of the day I will always follow them and go with their decision. I reason that the Lord is going to give clear direction through the people he has called into leadership. He has not called me there so I will follow those he has called.

I have in the past been involved in a messy end to the ministry of a pastor. I didn't acquit myself well. Never again do I want to contribute to disunity in the body of Christ. Instead, as far as it depends on me, I want to be one who brings about unity. If someone insists on falling out with me, I will keep forgiving and praying blessing on them – it takes two to cause disunity and I refuse to let it happen.

Standing firm

We noted earlier that the issue of the devil is the one that can do us the most damage but is the easiest to resolve. James 4:7 says, 'Submit to God. Resist the devil and he will flee from you.' As long as you are submitting to God, if you then resist the devil he has no choice but to flee. That applies to every Christian, no matter how weak and feeble you feel or how short a time you have been a Christian. In the third book in the series we will look more at how to do this in practice using The Steps To Freedom In Christ. In particular, we will look at escaping from those cycles where we sin, confess, then go and do it again...and again. We will see that we need to do more than simply confess to God that we did wrong. We must also resist the devil so that he flees from us. Then, in order to stay free, we need to identify the lies we were believing that made us get into the sin in the first place so that we can renew our minds to the truth of God's Word and not fall for them again.

The classic passage on living in victory over Satan is Ephesians 6:11–20 where Paul describes the armour that God provides to enable us to stand firm against his attacks. Let's look at the first couple of verses:

> *Finally, be strong in the Lord and in his mighty power. Put on the full armour of God so that you can take your stand against the devil's schemes. For our struggle is not against flesh and blood, but against the rulers, against the authorities, against the powers of this dark world and against the spiritual forces of evil in the heavenly realms. Therefore put on the full armour of God, so that when the day of evil comes, you may be able*

> *to stand your ground, and after you have done everything, to stand.*

You would think that a soldier's job was to attack the enemy, to hunt down these dark spiritual powers and dispose of them. However, Paul exhorts us not so much to attack but to 'stand'. The armour Paul describes is defensive armour. When he comes, for example, to the 'sword of the Spirit', he could have chosen a word describing a long attacking sword or even the Roman soldier's attacking javelin, but he did not. Instead he chose a word for a short defensive sword. The 'shield of faith' is for defence and, in fact, relies on our being alongside others. Divisions of Roman soldiers used to link their shields above them and around them so that they looked a little like a tortoise as they advanced together – whatever the enemy threw at them, it would simply bounce off. Like Roman soldiers, we are impregnable if we stand together in unity with our shields linked.

The key phrase perhaps is 'after you have done everything, to stand'. The sense is that if we do the things that we have the responsibility to do, Satan hasn't got a chance. He is already defeated and will simply have to flee before us. We are already 'more than conquerors' (Romans 8:37), so we simply have to defend ourselves against an enemy in his death throes. Yes, he will try his best to knock us off course, but he can't unless we let him. We have everything we need to withstand him – to quench *every* burning arrow he fires at us.

Why not spend some time now looking at the rest of that passage, understanding everything the Lord has given you to defend yourself? Note that the very first thing you put on is the belt of truth. Truth is fundamental and enables you to stand against the devil's deception. In this picture of the Roman soldier's armour, the belt is what held everything else together. The breastplate of righteousness (i.e. knowing that you are a saint, holy and righteous before God) stands against the devil's accusations. Allowing God's peace to rule in your heart (see

Colossians 3:15) will keep you from slipping. With the shield of faith you can extinguish not just some but 'all of the flaming arrows of the evil one' (Ephesians 6:16). The helmet of salvation – knowing the glorious truth that you are saved – will enable you to stand against Satan's assault on your mind, where the primary battle is taking place. Then there is the sword of the Spirit which is the 'word of God' – interestingly, the word Paul uses here for 'word' refers not to a written word but to a spoken word. There is a sense that speaking out the Word of God boldly is highly effective in our battle with the enemy – particularly significant, perhaps, in the light of our comments earlier that the enemy cannot read your thoughts: we need to speak out the Word of God if we want him to hear us.

What does it mean to 'put on the armour of God'? It's certainly more than saying a prayer every day along the lines of, 'I put on the belt of truth' and so on. There would be no point saying a prayer like that if you did not also make a firm commitment to truth. You put on the belt of truth by making a decision to commit yourself to truth and living accordingly. You lift up the shield of faith by making a decision to act according to what God has said reality is like rather than acting according to what the world, the flesh or the devil tells you.

After Paul has listed the various pieces of defensive armour, he says (verse 18): 'And pray in the Spirit on all occasions with all kinds of prayers and requests. With this in mind, be alert and always keep on praying for all the saints.' The armour allows us to stand our ground. We then take ground back from the enemy through prayer.

Our Enemies: The Flesh

We now come to the flesh, the third of our enemies. It comes at us from inside and in many ways is the most pernicious. However, as we shall see, we can expect to triumph over it nevertheless.

What is the flesh?

Adam and Eve were created with physical bodies with certain instincts and urges – to eat, to drink, to fall in love, to have sexual fulfilment and so on. Before they sinned, the way they managed those urges was healthy and pleasing to God. They could have chosen to overindulge but they had God's Spirit within them and they did not. That makes perfect sense because, if you had the amazing relationship with God that they had, why ever would you want to look elsewhere for comfort or gratification?

When they sinned, however, they died spiritually so no longer had God's Spirit within them or that relationship with God. They also began to experience physical death. In their case it took hundreds of years for their once-perfect bodies to decay and die, but die they did. Whereas before they were able to keep those bodily urges healthy and pleasing to God, once God's Spirit was removed they became a problem.

This was demonstrated when God gave his people a set of rules to govern their lives: 'the Law'. Paul says that in itself the Law was perfect – there was nothing wrong with it whatsoever. However, not a single person was able to keep it. Why not? Because everyone was weakened by 'the flesh' (Romans 8:3).

At its most basic, the term 'flesh' refers to our physical bodies and by extension to the instincts and urges that they have. You could perhaps sum up the biblical concept of the flesh by saying it is 'the urge to do what comes naturally to a fallen human being'.

'Flesh' is an unfamiliar word to the modern ear in this context, but it's exactly what the original Bible text says. The Greek word used in the New Testament (*sarx*) was the word used to describe, for example, meat you would buy from a butcher or the flesh on your leg. Many modern Bible translations do not translate the word 'flesh' literally but interpret it and use a phrase such as 'sinful nature' or 'old nature' (though you will normally find a footnote explaining what they have done). I understand why they do that – using a direct translation without explanation would not make a great deal of sense to modern readers. However, I find the use of the term 'nature' unhelpful because, as we have seen, Christians definitely do not any longer have a sinful nature but share God's nature. Deep down inside at the most fundamental level of our nature and identity, we are now holy and righteous. A phrase such as 'sinful tendency' might do the job better. It accurately conveys the concept that we have something inside us that pulls us towards sin without implying that we ourselves are back in the position of being fundamentally sinful. For the sake of clarity, however, I am going to stick with the literal translation 'flesh'.

The way the term is used in the New Testament encompasses these natural instincts and urges, but it is also used in a wider sense. Paul says this:

> Those who live according to the flesh have their minds on the things of the flesh but those who live according to the Spirit have their minds on the things of the Spirit, for the mind of the flesh is death, and the mind of the Spirit is life and peace; because the mind of the flesh is hostile to God.

(ROMANS 8:5–7A, MY TRANSLATION)

We see that the flesh is very much part of the battle going on for our minds. It comprises thoughts that come from inside us which are hostile to God and his Word but which become our 'default' ways of thinking and, therefore, behaving. We will automatically go with these thoughts, patterns and habits unless we take active steps not to.

The flesh pulls us away from truth and towards sin. There is no sense that our actual flesh (in terms of our physical body) is in any way evil but the urges that come from it are constantly pushing us towards evil.

A great deal changed for us when we became Christians. But not everything. For a start, we did not get a new body. I don't know about you, but mine is in considerably worse shape than when I first became a Christian! I can, however, take comfort from the fact that one day I'm going to get a brand-new body (see 1 Corinthians 15:42). Another thing that did not change was the flesh, a concept that, as we have seen, is very much linked to our physical body. Although we have it for now, one day when we get new bodies it will be gone. There is, however, a difference. Whereas before we had no real choice but to follow the urges of the flesh, now we do not have to.

1 Corinthians 2:14 – 3:3 describes three different types of person and will help us understand our relationship with the flesh:

The natural man does not accept the things that come from the Spirit of God, for they are foolishness to him, and he cannot understand them, because they are spiritually discerned.

The 'natural man' describes someone who is not yet a Christian, who is physically alive but remains spiritually dead and separated from God. This person still has those God-given needs for significance, security and acceptance but is living independently from God, and their actions and choices are dictated by the flesh. Paul now talks about a Christian:

> *The spiritual man makes judgments about all things, but he himself is not subject to any man's judgment: 'For who has known the mind of the Lord that he may instruct him?' But we have the mind of Christ.*

The Christian is a 'spiritual man' because his spirit is now alive. Through faith in Christ he has become a brand-new creation. His spirit is now reconnected to God and the Holy Spirit now lives in him. Although the flesh is pulling him towards sin, he chooses instead to respond to the impetus he receives from the Holy Spirit. He has the mind of Christ. He is gradually renewing the mind, where the battle is taking place, by getting rid of the old patterns of thinking and replacing them with truth.

So we have Christians and not-yet-Christians. You would think that that would cover everyone. However, Paul says that the Corinthian Christians fall into a third category:

> *Brothers, I could not address you as spiritual but as fleshly – mere infants in Christ. I gave you milk, not solid food, for you were not yet ready for it. Indeed, you are still not ready. You are still fleshly. For since there is jealousy and quarrelling among you, are you not fleshly? Are you not acting like mere men?*

Paul was unable to talk to them at the level of 'spiritual people' even though they were Christians. Instead he had to talk to them on a 'fleshly' level. They were Christians but they were consistently following the impetus of the flesh. The evidence for this was the obvious division among them.

It would be lovely if, when we became Christians, we were able to delete all those old ways of thinking in the same way we can delete old files on our computers and instantly replace them with new default ways of thinking that were in line with what is actually true. Unfortunately, there is no mechanism to do that and, unless we take steps to deal with the flesh, as Christians we will think and react in much the same way as before. So it is perfectly possible for a Christian, though made spiritually alive, to follow the flesh so that their daily life to all intents and purposes is indistinguishable from that of a non-Christian.

Just as you tell a tree by its fruit, you can tell whether you are walking by the Spirit or by the flesh by the fruit in your life. If you are being led by the Spirit, your life will be increasingly marked by love, joy, peace, patience, kindness, goodness, faithfulness, gentleness, and self-control (Galatians 5:22–23).

If you are living according to your flesh, that too will become evident in your life – Galatians 5:19–21 lists the type of fruit you can expect to see, including, for example, sexual sin, idolatry (worshipping things above God), hatred, discord, jealousy, anger and selfish ambition.

If we consistently follow the flesh, we will not be able to grow into fruitful disciples. We will not become the people God wants us to be. This is not a question of our salvation but of working out our salvation throughout the rest of our lives.

Tactics of the flesh

The way the flesh works is very straightforward. It establishes negative (and untrue) thought patterns in us. Then it tries to make these thought patterns more and more ingrained until they become 'strongholds'. A stronghold is a deeply entrenched flesh pattern that gives the enemy a lot of scope to influence our thinking. The flesh constantly pushes us to go with the default ways of thinking that it has established rather than follow the guidance of the Holy Spirit.

Tactic 1: Establish negative (and untrue) thought patterns

Most of our flesh habits are established in our early years but new negative thought patterns can be built into our thinking at any time, even when we are Christians and adults.

When we came into the world, we were physically alive but spiritually dead. We had very little programmed into our minds. As we grew up, independent of God, we learned to react in certain ways, to 'cope' in certain ways, to think in certain ways. We may, for example, have learned to cope with frightening situations by running away and hiding. Our tendency now as adults when confronted by something scary will probably be to bury our heads in the sand and hope it will all go away. On the other hand, we may have found that confronting the scary person or situation worked for us. Now as adults we will tend to be somewhat confrontational in the way we deal with others.

The flesh is not made up just of ways of coping. It also consists of negative thought patterns about God, ourselves or other people that come from negative experiences. For example, perhaps a little thought is planted in our mind by something that happens to us – maybe we are bullied or someone says something negative about us ('You're useless', 'You're a failure', 'You're ugly'). Perhaps we've believed it for so long that it becomes part of our lives and we can't imagine ever getting over it.

Satan works through the flesh and much of his agenda for our lives consists of setting up situations and scenarios that are designed to push us towards developing new unhelpful flesh patterns. When these are developed he wants them to become more and more ingrained so that they just feel like part of us and we can't imagine acting any other way.

What are some of the ways in which flesh patterns are formed?

Environment

The primary way we develop fleshly thinking is from our environment, particularly as we grow up. This is just like the way in which we simply absorb our worldview from the world around us.

I have two daughters and you will not be surprised to learn that they speak English. But if they had been brought up in a French home they would speak French. Just as we pick up things like language from our environment, we also pick up values and ways of behaving. We tend to discipline our children in the way we were disciplined. We tend to value what our peers value. Our family, community, schools, friends all had an effect – we absorbed ways of thinking and behaving from those around us, including ways of coping with the pressures of life independently of God.

We all had specific elements in our environment that would have predisposed us to pick up certain flesh patterns. Perhaps our parents tended to have outbursts of anger. Chances are we do too.

Perversion of natural urges

I heard recently that the number of websites that feature sex with children has quadrupled in five years. That reminded me of the depressing picture of humankind since the Fall that Paul paints at the beginning of his letter to the Roman church. He says that because people turned their backs on God, he 'gave them over in the sinful desires of their hearts to sexual impurity for the degrading of their bodies with one another' (Romans 1:24) and he 'gave them over to a depraved mind, to do what ought not to be done. They have become filled with every kind of wickedness, evil, greed and depravity' (Romans 1:28–29).

There are many such depressing statistics around sex. Apparently a quarter of men aged twenty-five to forty-nine regularly access 'adult websites' and, as previously noted, half the guests at major hotels use pay-per-view porn.

God created sex as an expression of intimate love in

the context of a life-long relationship between a man and a woman. How can something so beautiful have become so corrupted? It's down to the flesh. If left unchecked, it takes the urges and instincts that God built into our bodies and makes them in effect objects of worship in their own right. Instead of sexual intimacy being a way for me to show deep love to that special other person given to me by God, it becomes a means of self-gratification. The sexual act becomes an end in itself. The problem, of course, is that it was not designed for that and does not satisfy if used in that way. The result is that people looking for self-gratification tend to find themselves going down a path that leads to ever more perverted forms of sex.

The same thing happens with food, which was created to nourish our bodies. The flesh wants to establish it as an end in itself so that we become obsessed with eating or with the feeling of comfort that eating some types of food produces in our brain. The flesh wants us to use alcohol and other drugs in the same way. If the flesh had its way, we would increasingly cast off restraint in these areas in a futile search for fulfilment.

Giving in to temptation

Flesh patterns are formed when we give in to temptation. They become strongholds when we repeatedly give in to the same temptation.

Satan, of course, is the tempter and every temptation is an attempt to get us to live independently of God. The basis for temptation is usually our legitimate needs for significance, security and acceptance. The question is: are those needs going to be met by responding to the world, the flesh and the devil, or are they going to be met by God who promises to 'meet all your needs according to his glorious riches in Christ Jesus' (Philippians 4:19)?

Satan has observed your behaviour over the years and he knows where you are vulnerable, and that's where he will attack. Your temptations will be unique to your area of vulnerability.

Tempting thoughts that are not dealt with straight away lead on to actions. Repeating the action will result in a habit. Exercising the habit long enough produces a stronghold.

Traumatic experiences

Traumatic experiences can set up deeply entrenched flesh patterns because of their intensity. Living through a divorce, experiencing a death in the home or undergoing abuse might do that. Even brief one-off events such as a violent attack or viewing a horror film might have that effect.

When I was seventeen, one of my best friends was involved in a serious car crash and was expected to die. He ended up in a coma for four months and eventually made a good recovery. It was some years later that I realized that this one-off event had set up a stronghold in my thinking. The little thought, 'That could have been me' took hold and led to my being much more fearful than I would otherwise have been. Once I realized what had happened, I was able to dismantle the stronghold.

We'll talk in the third book in this series about how we can walk free from difficult events in the past. For now, however, I simply want to point out one crucial thing. It is not the traumatic experience itself that produces a stronghold, but the lies we believe as a result of it. In other words, it is not inevitable that a particular experience will set up a stronghold: in some people it will, in others it won't. Neither is it inevitable that, just because you have experienced a particular event or set of circumstances, you need to remain affected by it.

For example, if you were abused, you may well have come to see yourself as a victim – helpless, never able to stand up for yourself and take hold of truth. That may have been true of you at one time. But it's not true any more. You are a child of God who can do anything through Christ.

A mental stronghold is a lie based on past experiences that can be torn down in Christ. You can go back to those events and process them again from the position of who you are *now* – a child of God. The truth is that no Christian, no matter how bad their past experiences, has to remain a victim, because we are new creations in Christ. God does not change our past. He does, however, set us free from it.

Tactic 2: Establish strongholds

As we have seen, when a flesh habit becomes particularly entrenched, it becomes a 'stronghold'. The word means a castle or a fortress. It is found only once in the New Testament (2 Corinthians 10:4), so it would not be sensible to build a whole theology around it. However, these particularly entrenched flesh patterns that are not based on what is really true seem to provide Satan with a defensive fortification in our thinking from which he can more effectively influence us.

Ed Silvoso defines a stronghold as 'A mind-set impregnated with hopelessness that causes us to accept as unchangeable situations that we know are contrary to the will of God.' Neil Anderson says, 'Strongholds are mental habit patterns of thought that are not consistent with God's Word.'

I would add that a stronghold can often be spotted when you come across something you know you should do but don't seem able to, or something you know you shouldn't do but don't feel able to stop.

Think of a stronghold this way. Let's say after it rains you drive a Land Rover across a field – it would create some ruts. If you do that every day for some time, the ruts will get more and more established and after a while you won't even have to steer. The Land Rover will follow the ruts. In fact, any attempt to steer out of the ruts will be met with resistance.

If we don't know how to tear down these mental strongholds we may well give up and conclude (wrongly), 'That's just the way I am – I can't change'; 'I occasionally have fits of anger: well, that's just me'; or 'I'm just very shy – I can't change'. Feelings of inferiority, insecurity and inadequacy are other examples of strongholds because they are simply not true. No child of God is inferior or inadequate. No Christian need feel insecure when Jesus has made a firm promise that no one can take us out of his hand (John 10:28).

So, the flesh is all about establishing negative, untrue thought patterns in us and taking them deeper and deeper so that they provide an ever more secure base for the enemy to influence our thinking. If you have a stronghold of inadequacy, for example, every time the Lord encourages you to step out in faith and exercise a gift that he has given you, it is relatively easy for the enemy to 'press your buttons' and fill your mind with thoughts of 'I couldn't do that' or 'People won't accept me exercising that gift', and the chances are that you will (wrongly) agree with him and miss out on an opportunity to grow as a disciple. Once you tear down that stronghold and know the truth that you are absolutely not inferior, then you can choose to take a deep gulp and a step of faith and allow the Lord to use you.

The effects of strongholds

The problem with strongholds is that they deflect you from the truth. If your belief system is not in line with what is true, then your feelings are likely to be all over the place.

A dear friend of mine had suffered a lot of rejection in her life. When she went to church on a Sunday this set her up to feel that others did not like her. Unless the pastor made a really special effort to greet her warmly and give her a hug, she felt rejected. On the occasions when he simply smiled and said a quick 'hello', all of those feelings of rejection from the past flowed over her once more. The truth, of course, is that he simply needed to concentrate on what he was about to say to the church or he was just digesting last night's curry! A stronghold will cause you to feel rejection when you are not rejected or helpless to change when actually you are not. You will live your life acting on false information.

A woman came up to me after I had been teaching about our new identity in Christ. Tears were rolling down her cheeks and she said over and over again with great joy, 'I'm not inferior!' She explained that her older brother had always been the clever one and that she had grown up with a profound sense of being inferior. Many people over the years had told her that she was not inferior but that had not changed how she felt and how she acted. During that session the Word of God had opened her eyes and she saw herself as she really was. A stronghold had been torn down. If she continued to reject the lie that she was inferior, her feelings would eventually change and her perception of herself would be based on the truth that she is indeed a child of God.

Strongholds lead us to make wrong decisions. Every day we have to make a choice between doing things God's way and doing things our own way influenced by the world, the flesh and the devil. To live a truly free life in Christ we have to know, and choose to believe, what God says.

When you know that God is a loving Father full of wisdom who knows what is best for you, why ever would you not want to do things the way he suggests? Because of strongholds. They lead us to try to work things out for ourselves, to 'lean on our own understanding' (Proverbs 3:5). They convince us that God is not loving or that he does not love us. They predispose us not to trust him or anyone else. In short, strongholds will lead us to make bad choices because they are based on false information.

A stronghold will predispose us to ignore the 'Danger' signs that God has posted, making us think that we know best how we can feel significant, secure and accepted.

We are anything but helpless in this struggle. In Christ, we have the choice and ability every day to renew our minds by choosing God's way instead of leaning on our own understanding. You control the outcome of this daily battle for your mind.

Our defence against the flesh

Resolve spiritual conflicts

As we have seen, Satan works through the flesh and strongholds can give him a significant point of influence in our thinking. The first thing many computers do when they are switched on is scan for viruses. The first thing we need to do is scan for any point of influence we have given Satan in the past through sin and remove it by repenting, as previously described.

Once the footholds are removed, our flesh patterns are simply habitual ways of thinking that we have learned – and habits can be changed. If we do not deal with the enemy's influence first, we will struggle to renew our minds and to get out of sin–confess cycles.

Once we have dealt with any unresolved spiritual conflicts and committed ourselves to believe truth, no matter what we feel, we are genuinely free to make a choice every day either to obey the promptings of the flesh or the promptings of the Holy Spirit.

Learn to resist temptation

Although we constantly face temptation, we don't ever have to give in to it:

> No temptation has seized you except what is common to man. And God is faithful; he will not let you be tempted beyond what you can bear. But when you are tempted, he will also provide a way out so that you can stand up under it.
>
> (1 CORINTHIANS 10:13)

I used to get really irritated with that verse because it didn't seem that there was a way out. 'Where is it then, God?' I would shout. So where is it?

God has provided a way of escape from all temptation and

it is right at the beginning of the process – when the tempting thought first comes into your mind. That's your opportunity to 'take captive every thought to make it obedient to Christ' (2 Corinthians 10:5). This is akin to recognizing the schemes of the enemy against us. When we understand how he tends to tempt us, we can be alert and ready for the tempting thought, and when it comes we will recognize it for what it is and take appropriate action.

Suppose that pornography is a particular vulnerability for you. You need to fill the car with petrol and there are two petrol stations nearby. One of them has a shop attached to it which sells pornography, the other does not. Which one are you going to go to? Your chance to make the right choice comes when you are first presented with this choice, when the thought first enters your head. As soon as you decide to go towards the place where they sell pornography, you can rationalize as much as you like ('Well, the petrol is usually cheaper and I need some other things from the shop too'), but in fact, whether you admit it to yourself or not, you know very well that you are being drawn to look at the pornography. At that point your chances of turning around are diminishing rapidly. In fact, you will be sexually stimulated long before you get there just by thinking about where you are going and why. The tempter is working on your mind before you even look at the pornography. As soon as you do look at it, of course, he becomes the accuser and puts untrue thoughts into your mind such as, 'Call yourself a Christian? Surely God can't still love you after yet another failure, can he?' The answer? To reject the tempting thought to go to that petrol station as soon as it appears, because you have learned to recognize what's really going on.

A further defence against temptation is to understand how devastating the effects of sin are. Most married people will at some point face a temptation to flirt with an attractive member of the opposite sex. It may seem harmless. However, it can also give the enemy an opportunity to introduce tempting thoughts into your mind ('My wife isn't as exciting as she is...'; 'It's so long since any man gave me that kind of attention'), and in some cases these take root and it can eventually lead to a full-blown affair. If, like I have, you have sat down with someone while they tell their unsuspecting wife that they have been having an affair, you will know how absolutely devastating the outcome of this sin is. The pain caused to spouses and children is enormous. It can take many years for people to recover, if indeed they ever do. All because someone was looking in the wrong place for their legitimate need for acceptance to be met – when God was meeting it 100 per cent all the time. Having witnessed first hand the devastation caused by an affair, I am much more careful about that kind of temptation in my own life. Seeing through the deception of temptation to the mess and bondage it inevitably leads to if we fall for it makes us much more likely to recognize the tempting thought and throw it out as soon as it appears.

> *Flee from sexual immorality. All other sins a man commits are outside his body, but he who sins sexually sins against his own body. Do you not know that your body is a temple of the Holy Spirit, who is in you, whom you have received from God? You are not your own; you were bought at a price. Therefore honour God with your body.* (1 CORINTHIANS 6:18–20)

The picture that gives me is of Joseph, who turned tail and ran when Potiphar's wife tried to seduce him (Genesis 39:12). The sins of the flesh are so tempting that we have to train ourselves to recognize them and run from them because we do not want to grieve the Holy Spirit by defiling the temple that our body now is.

It can be helpful to think of your mind as an airport where you are the air-traffic controller. A lot of thoughts ask for permission to land. But you have complete control over which will land and which will be turned away. You have to decide right at the outset, however. The moment you give a tempting thought permission to land, the chances of your being able to turn it away reduce significantly. This is what the Bible calls 'taking every thought captive' (2 Corinthians 10:5). It requires effort and a constant commitment to truth.

Our relationship with sin

It may be helpful at this point to clarify our relationship with sin. We could define sin as an action or attitude whereby we rebel against God and surrender to the power of evil. The world, the flesh and the devil are constantly trying to push us towards an act of rebellion against God through sin in thought and action in order to give them influence in our lives.

Paul sometimes writes as though sin were a person (e.g. Romans 7:8, 'But sin, seizing the opportunity afforded by the commandment, produced in me every kind of covetous desire'). Should we include sin as an enemy in its own right alongside the world, the flesh and the devil? When Paul personifies sin in this way, he seems in effect to be using it as a generic term for the world, the flesh and the devil. They are all sin. To use the verse just quoted, they are all trying to produce covetous desires in us.

Every Christian knows what it is like to be caught in a sin. It starts out feeling very appealing. We fall for the lie that it will meet our needs, forgetting that they are already fully met in Christ. We give in to temptation. Before we know it, we are drawn back there again and again. Ultimately, it is as if sin is our master. We don't enjoy it any more but we don't seem able to stop. It promised freedom but instead it has turned out as bondage.

Paul says that there is a 'law of sin' (Romans 7:23). Whenever we want to do something good, up pops sin in the shape of the world, the flesh and the devil to push us towards rebellion against the truth. He says that sin used to be our master and that we were 'slaves to sin' (Romans 6:20) but that it has no power over us any more. He says its power is broken in the life of a Christian. In fact, he goes so far as to tell us that we are to consider ourselves to be alive to God and dead to sin (Romans 6:11). It is not, of course, the 'considering' that makes us dead to sin – we consider ourselves dead to sin because we are! Paul is helping us to grasp the truth that we died with Christ and that his death ended our relationship with sin. Death always ends relationships and in this case it ended our relationship with sin.

The big question for many Christians is, how can we defeat the law of sin? The good news is that in one sense you don't have to defeat sin because Christ has already done it. There is no point trying to beat something that is already defeated. We simply need to know the truth.

An illustration may be helpful here. What Paul calls 'the law of sin and death', whereby sin pops up the moment we want to do good, is still operative. How can you overcome a law that still works?

Can you fly? If you have ever tried, you will have discovered that the law of gravity is another law that is still operative. Every time you tried to get off the ground, up popped gravity to keep you down. However, if you get into an aeroplane, you can fly. Even though the law of gravity is still working, the 'plane's forward thrust and the law of aerodynamics combine to overcome the law of gravity. So how do you overcome a law that is still effective? You overcome it by a more powerful law. Yes, the law of sin is still effective – we have the world, the flesh and the devil pulling us constantly towards sin. But we died to sin and a greater law now operates: 'Through Christ Jesus the law of the Spirit of life set me free from the law of sin and death' (Romans 8:2).

The law that is now at work in me as a child of God is the law of the Spirit of life, and it is far greater than the law of sin and death. Whereas before I had no choice but to stay on the ground in my sin, now I can choose to fly above the law of sin and death! We will look at this in more detail in the third book in this series.

Walk by the Spirit

Perhaps the most important concept for us to grasp is that the flesh operates in direct opposition to the Holy Spirit and to his guidance. Galatians 5:17 says, 'For the flesh desires what is contrary to the Spirit, and the Spirit what is contrary to the flesh. They are in conflict with each other, so that you do not do what you want.'

If someone struggling with an addiction to alcohol – which is a stronghold – came to you for help, what advice would you give them? Ephesians 5:18 starts like this: 'Do not get drunk on wine, which leads to debauchery. Instead...' Before we look at what Paul says after 'Instead', consider for a moment what you would say. Do not get drunk but instead... What?

The great majority of programmes that deal with alcoholism have abstinence (i.e. not drinking) as their goal. They would say in effect, 'Do not get drunk but instead don't drink.' That is not, however, what Paul says. In fact, he gives us a revolutionary concept: 'Do not get drunk on wine, which leads to debauchery. Instead, be filled with the Spirit.'

A couple of years ago, I bought a new car. It was my first diesel model. A week or so after taking delivery, I went to fill the tank. My excuse is that I was tired but I ended up filling the tank with petrol rather than diesel. I realized halfway through and stopped filling and went and had a word with the man in the petrol station. He informed me that driving a diesel car with petrol in it was likely to cause enormous damage to the engine. The petrol would have to be drained and then the tank filled with diesel.

If we pour the wrong fuel into the petrol tank, the answer is not merely to stop pouring. The complete answer is to stop pouring in the wrong fuel that ruins the engine, and then drain the tank and start pouring in the right fuel. If we are living wrongly, the answer is not to stop living, the answer is to start living rightly.

If you are giving in to the flesh and following its impulses, the answer is to choose instead to follow the impulses of the Holy Spirit. One of the roles of the Holy Spirit is to 'guide you into all truth' (John 16:13), whereas the flesh wants to guide you into bondage.

The answer to the flesh is not so much to try not to do the negative thing ('don't drink', 'don't have lustful thoughts', 'don't gorge yourself') – the key principle is this: 'Live by the Spirit and you will not gratify the desires of the flesh' (Galatians 5:16). That's quite a categorical statement. It's also revolutionary. When we choose to walk by the Spirit, we will not gratify the desires of the flesh. Fact.

What does walking by the Spirit actually mean? We have seen that the word 'flesh' implies an association with our physical bodies. Now that we are Christians, however, our bodies are 'a temple of the Holy Spirit' (1 Corinthians 6:19).

In Ephesians 5:18, which we have just looked at, when Paul says, 'Be filled with the Spirit', he uses a Greek tense which implies a continuous action. The verse could accurately be rendered, 'Go on and on being filled with the Spirit'. In other words, being filled with the Spirit is not a one-off event but something that we need to come back to again and again.

Walking by the Spirit, then, involves a conscious day-by-day decision to recognize that and to offer our bodies to God: 'I urge you, brothers, in view of God's mercy, to offer your bodies as living sacrifices, holy and pleasing to God – this is your spiritual act of worship' (Romans 12:1).

In my struggles with the ingrained flesh pattern of comfort eating, I find that simply reminding myself that my body is a temple of the Holy Spirit makes me think twice before pumping it full of junk food. I want to honour him in my body. It is his temple. I also find that when I am going through a time of struggle with the flesh, consciously offering my body as a living sacrifice at the beginning of the day is very helpful.

I am dedicating my body to the service of God rather than to my own selfish desires.

Walking by the Spirit is a supernatural thing, a day-by-day, moment-by-moment reliance on God himself, who has chosen to make his home in us. We depend completely on him for this. Left to ourselves, we would return to sin. But as we depend on him, he leads us in ways of righteousness. He enables us to make the right choices.

There are two extremes we want to avoid as we walk by the Spirit. Firstly, the freedom that Jesus won for us is not a licence to do whatever we want. Some think that freedom means we can cast off all the guidelines God has given to help us lead responsible lives. They reason that if their salvation is secure, it does not matter how they live.

Paul responds to this line of thinking in 1 Corinthians 6:12, quoting what he has heard others saying: '"Everything is permissible for me" – but not everything is beneficial. "Everything is permissible for me" – but I will not be mastered by anything.'

There is the crux of the matter. Yes, as a Christian you are free to do whatever you want. But if you simply follow the desires of the flesh, you will soon realize that that is not freedom at all. It is actually slavery. The real question to ask is not 'Can I do this?' but 'Can I *stop* doing it?' Paul points out that simply giving in to fleshly urges because we think there are no consequences is self-deception. You end up being mastered by the flesh and feeling unable to stop. In Romans 7 Paul describes what it feels like when you finally realize that you are caught in that kind of trap: 'miserable'.

When Jesus memorably spoke about true freedom, he said this: 'I tell you the truth, everyone who sins is a slave to sin. Now a slave has no permanent place in the family, but a son belongs to it forever. So if the Son sets you free, you will be free indeed' (John 8:34–36). The issue for him was slavery to sin. That is what he died to set you free from. Yes, you are free to go back into it, but why ever would you want to? Yes, you can do whatever you want to do, but why would you choose to go back to being a slave?

Secondly, we want to avoid thinking that we can reduce walking by the Spirit to a set of dos and don'ts. The Old Testament Law revealed how we would have to behave if we wanted to please God through behaviour – but nobody could live up to it. The point of the Law was to show us our need for Christ (Galatians 3:24). Yet so many of us, even as Christians, tend to live as if we still have to obey certain rules in order to be accepted by God or to be 'a good Christian'. However, 'If you are led by the Spirit, you are not under law' (Galatians 5:18). As we choose to walk by the Spirit, we are enabled to live a righteous life by faith.

Know where real comfort is found

This is what Jesus says about the Holy Spirit:

> And I will ask the Father, and he will give you another Counsellor [Comforter, Intercessor] to be with you forever – the Spirit of truth. The world cannot accept him, because it neither sees him nor knows him. But you know him, for he lives with you and will be in you. I will not leave you as orphans; I will come to you.   (JOHN 14:16–18)

The word Jesus uses (*parakletos*) to describe the Holy Spirit is a word that carries the meaning of one who comes alongside, one who consoles or comforts, one who counsels or is an advocate and one who intercedes. Jesus specifically says that he will not leave us as orphans, cut off from our true parent. The Holy Spirit fulfils that parenting role in our lives. He gives us advice, he consoles us and helps us with the pain we have picked up along the way, he prays for us.

Paul describes God as 'the God of all comfort' (2 Corinthians 1:3). What the flesh purports to offer us above everything else is comfort. It promises to make us feel better. We are much more susceptible to fall for it when we are feeling low.

The truth is that, although the flesh may give us a sort of temporary comfort (though it's more of a temporary blotting out of our negative emotions than genuine comfort), only God can really meet our deep need to be consoled and comforted. The great news is that he is always ready to do that in the person of the Holy Spirit.

When we understand that, we are much more likely to turn to him instead of to the flesh when we feel in need of that comfort.

Demolish strongholds

Do we have to put up with strongholds? No!

> For though we live in the world we do not wage war as the world does. The weapons we fight with are not the weapons of the world. On the contrary, they have divine power to demolish strongholds. We demolish arguments and every pretension that sets itself up against the knowledge of God, and we take every thought captive to make it obedient to Christ.
>
> (2 CORINTHIANS 10:3–5)

Once you have taken away any foothold of the enemy by repenting, a stronghold is nothing more than a habitual way of thinking and behaving. If you have believed a lie, you can renounce that lie and choose the truth instead.

We mentioned earlier that a stronghold is like a Land Rover creating deep ruts in a field so that it becomes difficult to steer out of them. But you can steer out of the ruts of habitual faulty thinking by making a sustained effort over a period of time. If you've learned something wrongly, you can relearn it. If you have programmed your computer badly, you can reprogram it. But you have to want to. You have to choose to. And you have to know that it is possible for you to be 'transformed by the renewing of your mind' (Romans 12:2).

Psychologists say that it takes around six weeks (or forty days, if you like a good biblical number!) to form a habit or break a habit. I recommend a strategy called 'stronghold-busting' to you. First of all, you need to determine the lie you have been believing (any way you are thinking that is not in line with what God says about you in the Bible). In doing this, ignore what you feel but commit yourself wholeheartedly to God's truth. For example, you might realize that you have been believing the lie: 'Eating brings lasting comfort'.

Then, find as many Bible verses as you can that state the truth and write them down. Some good Bible software (or a helpful pastor) will come in useful. Write a prayer or declaration based on this formula:

- I renounce the lie that...
- I announce the truth that...

Finally, read the Bible verses and say the prayer/declaration every day for forty days, all the time reminding yourself that God is truth and that if he has said it, it really is true for you. Don't worry if you miss a day or two (this is not a legalistic ritual), but do persevere until you have completed a total of forty days. In fact, you may wish to go on longer, and you will almost certainly want to come back and do it again at some point in the future.

Remember that it takes time to demolish a stronghold and get rid of negative thinking. Just because the thoughts recur, doesn't mean it's not working – it's whether or not you choose to believe the thoughts that is important.

Ed Silvoso tells of how a pastor friend of his watched a concrete wall being demolished. It withstood ten, then fifteen, then thirty, then thirty-five blows with no visible sign of being weakened. That's how it can feel as you work through a Stronghold-Buster day after day. However, each day you renounce the lie and commit yourself to truth is making a difference. A wall might appear not to have been weakened right up to, say, thirty-seven swings of a demolition ball. However, sooner or later (say on the thirty-eighth swing), a few small cracks will appear. On the next swing these cracks will get bigger until, finally, the wall completely collapses. Even though only the final three swings appear to have had an effect, without all the previous ones, the wall would not have fallen. We will look further at this concept in the third book in the series.

One of the most frustrating things I encounter is Christians who start the process of renewing their mind using a Stronghold-Buster but do not finish. If I ask them why, they will often say, 'I stopped because it wasn't working.' I sometimes want to shake them and say, 'That is the whole point!' By definition, a stronghold will go on feeling true until it has been dismantled. In other words, the process will feel as if it is not working practically all the way through. Dismantling a stronghold involves persevering and making a choice every day to commit yourself to what God has said is true, which flies in the face of what your feelings and past experiences are telling you.

Here's an example of a Stronghold-Buster that I put together to help me with my weakness for comfort eating:

The lie: that overeating brings lasting comfort.

Proverbs 25:28: Like a city whose walls are broken down is a man who lacks self-control.

Galatians 5:16: So I say, live by the Spirit, and you will not gratify the desires of the sinful nature.

Galatians 5:22: But the fruit of the Spirit is love, joy, peace, patience, kindness, goodness, faithfulness, gentleness and self-control. Against such things there is no law. Those who belong to Christ Jesus have crucified the sinful nature with its passions and desires.

2 Corinthians 1:3–4: Praise be to the God and Father of our Lord Jesus Christ, the Father of compassion and the God of all comfort, who comforts us in all our troubles, so that we can comfort those in any trouble with the comfort we ourselves have received from God.

Psalm 63:4–5: I will praise you as long as I live, and in your name I will lift up my hands. My soul will be satisfied as with the richest of foods; with singing lips my mouth will praise you.

Psalm 119:76: May your unfailing love be my comfort.

Prayer: Lord, I renounce the lie that overeating brings lasting comfort. I announce the truth that you are the God of all comfort and that your unfailing love is my only legitimate and real comfort. I affirm that I now live by the Spirit and do not have to gratify the desires of the flesh. Whenever I feel in need of comfort, instead of turning to foods I choose to praise you and be satisfied as with the richest of foods. Fill me afresh with your Holy Spirit and live through me as I grow in self-control. Amen.

Tick off the days:

1	2	3	4	5	6	7	8	9	10
11	12	13	14	15	16	17	18	19	20
21	22	23	24	25	26	27	28	29	30
31	32	33	34	35	36	37	38	39	40

In the third book in this series we will look at further examples of Stronghold-Busters.

Freedom to choose

We will be battling the flesh until our dying day. However, as we get to understand our vulnerabilities and renew our minds, we can expect to see victory over it.

Remember the key principle: 'Live by the Spirit and you will not gratify the desires of the flesh' (Galatians 5:16). 'Where the Spirit of the Lord is, there is freedom' (2 Corinthians 3:17). Walking by the Spirit is genuine freedom and when we allow him to fill us, he will lead us in righteousness. The freedom that has been won for us is the freedom to choose, the freedom that Adam and Eve had originally. In any situation we can choose to walk by the Spirit rather than by the flesh.

Let me finish this chapter by telling you about a friend of mine who had a very difficult childhood in which he was largely ignored by his parents and sometimes abused by them. His father would often tell him that he was 'a useless waste of space' and that phrase stuck in his mind and became part of his flesh.

He became a Christian and later a pastor, but the pain from his past did not go away and he turned to alcohol to try to escape from it. It destroyed his marriage and his ministry. After years of alcoholism he got hold of the truth that the power of sin was broken in his life because of who he is as a child of God, and he walked away from the alcoholism, resolved his spiritual conflicts and found his freedom in Christ. He has now helped many others to find that same freedom.

Yet he tells me that there is not a day in his life when his flesh does not tell him that he is 'a useless waste of space'. The negative fleshly thought pattern established in the environment of his family home has not gone away. However, he has learned to make a choice every day simply not to listen to it – no matter how strongly it might come over – because he now knows that it is not true. He has demolished the stronghold.

Instead he makes a daily choice to listen to the promptings

More Than Conquerors

A little while ago I was privileged to stay in the home of a pastor whose church was hosting a conference I was speaking at. His young son invited me to play against him in a computer game. It seemed a fairly straightforward racing-car game. However, I couldn't get to grips with it. My car kept hitting walls, spinning off the track and, frequently, going the wrong way entirely. Occasionally, banks of missiles appeared out of nowhere and I was helpless to avoid them.

To the young lad's credit, he did not give up on me. Instead he spent some time – quite a lot of time, actually – explaining to me how this weird world worked. I learned that I had a 'booster' button that could accelerate me away from the dangers of the missiles. I understood how to steer in vaguely the right direction. Needless to say, he still thrashed me but at least I was able to complete a lap with some vestige of dignity.

The battle that we find ourselves in when we become Christians can seem a little like being plunged into a strange computer game where you don't know the rules or what is going to happen next. In this book I have simply tried to explain how it works, to demystify it, to point out that you and I are, as Paul says, 'more than conquerors' (Romans 8:37).

Let's remind ourselves of Sun Tzu's wise advice for battle:

If you know the enemy and know yourself, you need not fear the result of a hundred battles. If you know yourself but not the enemy, for every victory gained you will also suffer a defeat. If you know neither the enemy nor yourself, you will succumb in every battle.

Yes, we have no fewer than three enemies. Yes, each one of them appears formidable. However, we have weapons to defeat them all every time.

The *world* cannot overcome us because 'Everyone born of God overcomes the world' (1 John 5:4).

Even though *Satan* is real and unimaginably evil, he can only operate within God-given boundaries and, for the Christian, demonic issues are straightforward to resolve: 'Submit yourselves, then, to God. Resist the devil, and he will flee from you' (James 4:7).

We can expect to experience daily victory over the *flesh*: 'Live by the Spirit, and you will not gratify the desires of the flesh' (Galatians 5:16).

I hope that you now feel that you do indeed know your enemies and are excited to see that neither the flesh, the world nor the devil can stop you becoming all that God wants you to be.

My prayer is that you also know yourself better. You are, after all, holy through and through, seated with Christ at the right hand of the Father, far above all demonic spirits, and you have been given all power and authority to go into the world and make disciples. That makes you a much more formidable force in the battle than all of your enemies combined!

In the next book in this series we will look at how practically we can resolve the effects of the past and take hold of the freedom that Christ died to give us. For now, let me leave you with a couple of verses that, for me, sum up our amazing position in the battle we are in:

For in Christ all the fullness of the Deity lives in bodily form, and you are complete in him, who is the head over every power and authority. (COLOSSIANS 2:9–10)

Freedom **Freedom In**
Christ **Christ In The UK**

Church leaders – can we help you make disciples?

Although the Church may have made some *converts*, most will agree that we have made few real *disciples*. Far too many Christians struggle to take hold of basic biblical truth and *live it out*. It's not as if we lack excellent teaching programmes. It's more to do with people's ability to "connect" with truth. Or, as Jesus put it, "You will *know* the truth and the truth will set you free." (John 8:32)

Many churches in the UK now use the Freedom In Christ approach to help Christians make connections with truth and mature into fruitful disciples. It works well as: a church-wide discipleship programme using The Freedom In Christ Discipleship Course; a follow-up to introductory courses like Alpha; a cell equipping track; or a small group study.

If you are a UK church leader, we are at your disposal. We run a regular programme of conferences and training, and are always happy to offer advice.

Send for our catalogue

Send for our full colour catalogue of books, videos and audiocassettes. It includes resources for churches and for individuals (including children and young people and specialist areas such as depression and addiction).

Join the Freedom Fellowship

For those using the Freedom In Christ approach, the Freedom Fellowship provides advice on getting started in your church and regular news and encouragement.

For details of any of the above, see www.ficm.org.uk, e-mail info@ficm.org.uk or write to us at:
Freedom In Christ Ministries, PO Box 2842, READING RG2 9RT.

www.**ficm**.org.uk

Freedom In Christ Ministries is a company limited by guarantee (number 3984116) and a registered charity (number 1082555). It works by equipping local churches to help Christians claim their freedom in Christ and become fruitful disciples.